SVARA

Stories wait around to be told until someone tells them.

A single story does not exist in this world without a storyteller.

Each person, each place, each moment...

To tell a story is to breathe life into a story.

Let go of the desire to tell a story and the story will tell itself, through you.

Inhale this moment.

Exhale this story.

SVARA means voice.

A voice tells a story. Telling one person's story at a time, we create an impression of the place that is South India. The monumental task of telling these stories, the stories of a multitude of strangers who took us in, cared for us, and taught us about their home, is not lost on us as documentarians. We learned the depth of the privilege we were afforded upon entering into these in the form of the visual stories we created and now share with you.

The Brooks Institute Documentary Project to South India in 2008 and the resulting work in these pages is the culmination of a year's work by 20 students in the Visual Journalism, Professional Photography, Film & Video Production and Graphic Design programs. For seven weeks in late 2008, the documentarians created the raw materials, the photographs, videos, audio and written texts that became this book, a documentary film, a DVD, a website and several print exhibits.

Here in these pages the intimacy of daily life in South India is spoken freely and with conviction.

Paul Myers
Executive Producer
Faculty, Visual Journalism
Brooks Institute
April 2, 2009

CONTENTS

Book Designed & Edited by:

Adam Herrera, Lead Production Editor
Sybill Jecker, Lead Layout Designer
Courtney Black
Jennifer Homsher
Samantha Murphy
Amanda Reyes

Paul Myers, Executive Producer
Ellen Webber, Producer
Yoo Hwa Almaraz-Hwang, Graphic Artist

BrooksInstitute
PASSION. VISION. EXCELLENCE.

http://documentary.brooks.edu/india
©2009 Brooks Institute
27 Cota Street, Santa Barbara, CA 93101
All photos copyright of individual photographers.

Printed by V3 Corporation

ISBN: 978-0-9718622-7-2

Front cover: Photo by Samantha Murphy
Back cover: Photo by Jeff Johns

Right: Photo by Mia Shimabuku

TRADITI

HARVESTING THE SEA

By Cesare Naldi

In the state of Kerala, alongside the ever-expanding and developing modern fishing industry, some traditional fishing techniques are still practiced today.

Cochin, a city in Kerala, is one of India's four main fishing harbors. From sunrise to sunset, teams of fishermen haul enormous structures called Chinese fishing nets from the sea. These immense cantilevered nets can be 65 feet in width and are attached to a network of finger-like bamboo towers. It takes several men to hoist a single net from the sea, and more often than not, the effort outweighs the return. However, this fishing technique is so old

and peculiar that it has become a major tourist attraction in Cochin, providing the fishermen with extra income.

In the Keralan beach town of Kovalam, several small wooden catamarans leave from shore every morning at sunrise. Armed with a machete, a mask, and a small net, mussel fishermen jump from their catamarans into the sea to harvest their prize. They free dive at depths that vary from 10 to 20 feet for hours until their catamarans are nearly overflowing with mussels. On the beach, women wait patiently to carry the heavy catch to nearby markets.

ARTERIES OF KERALA

By Sybill Jecker

The backwaters are sometimes called the arteries of Kerala. Historically, these waterways that connect the freshwater lakes to the Arabian Sea have been used to transport both goods and people from one location to another throughout the state. In addition, the brackish water provides a unique environment for fish, wildlife and agriculture. For the people who live in these backwater regions, every aspect of their life revolves around this natural resource, from bathing and eating to fueling the economies that support their families. Homes are situated along the waterways and temple singers can be heard up and down the canals in the evenings.

Recently, the backwaters of Kerala have become a popular tourist destination with the introduction of touring houseboats by innovator Babu Varghese. As the development of roads reduced the use of the backwaters for transporting goods, boat craftsmen and operators found themselves out of work. Varghese's idea of converting the rice paddy boats of the past to luxurious vessels of comfort and relaxation, combined with offering traditional Keralan meals, has provided the boating industry with ongoing work and many travelers from around the world with a spectacular view of the backwater scenery that is exclusive to this South Indian state.

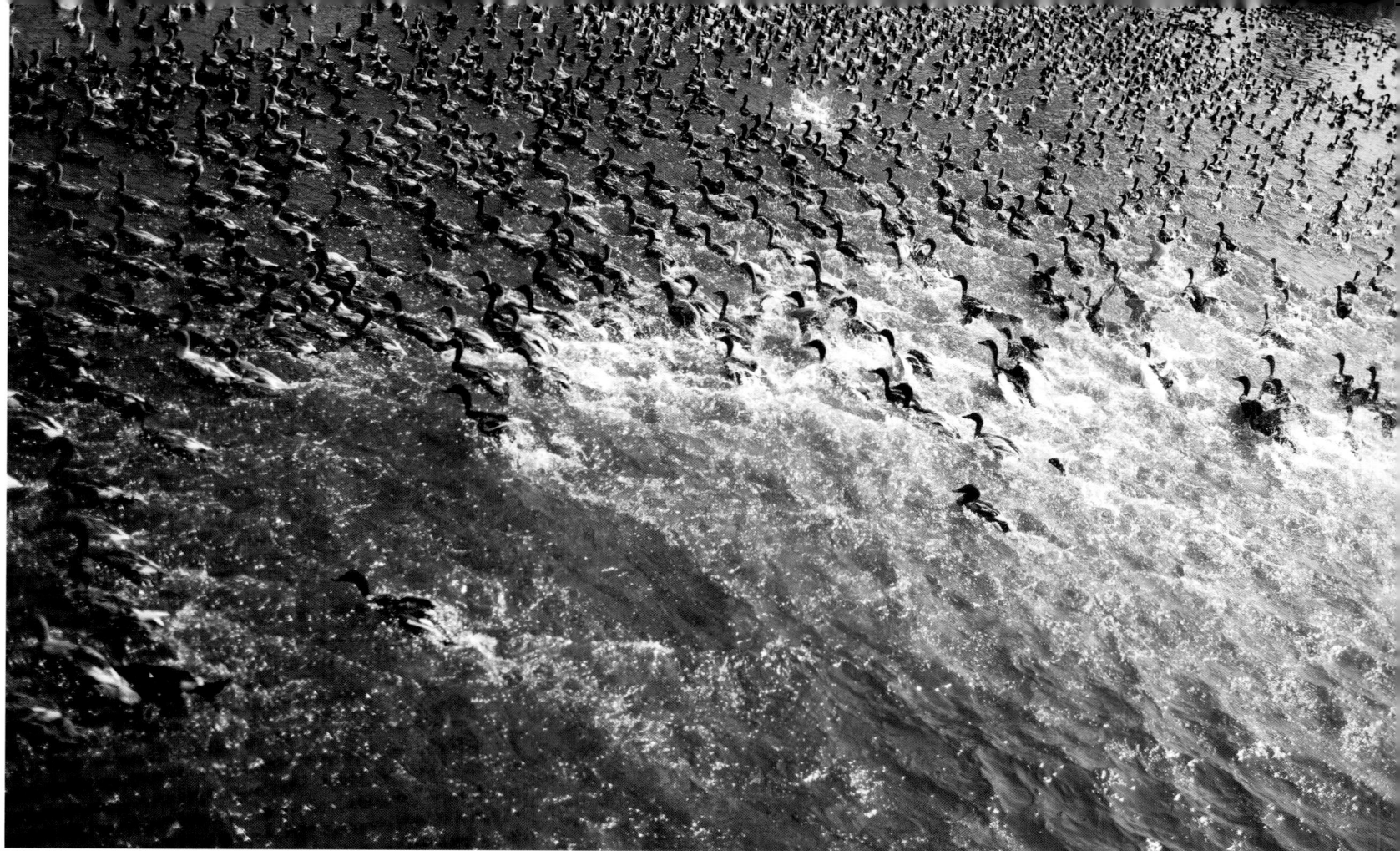

INTEGRITY

By Alana Fickes

Hand washing garments and household linens is a
tradition in India, where large appliances in homes
are rare, especially in the backwaters of Kerala.

FROM BEESWAX TO BRONZE

By Jennifer Homsher

Chola bronzes, made from lost wax bronze casting, originated during the great Chola dynasty, which ruled Tanjavor, Kerala, and the state of Tamil Nadu between the 9th and 12th centuries. The process begins with modeling a statue from beeswax, which is then packed in clay and allowed to harden for several days. The clay mold is then heated and the wax melts, leaving a negative space in the clay.

Next, liquid bronze is poured into the mold and left to cool. Later, the clay is broken away and the metal statue is filed and polished until the finished product is ready.

N. Kathirvel learned the art of lost wax bronze casting from his father, a craft that has been passed down through the generations. Formerly creating traditional statues for temples and home altars, Kathirvel's

family now caters to Western tourists by producing smaller, more portable statues. This has allowed for a faster turn around and more predictable income for his family.

CARVED FROM STONE

By Nicole Vinisky

The art of stone carving has been flourishing in the small town of Mamallapuram in Tamil Nadu, for thousands of years. Centuries ago, artists and craftsmen were commissioned to carve huge religious icons and stories out of the cliff faces and boulders that are scattered throughout the town. Today, Mamallapuram is home to the largest number of stone carvers in all of India.

Everything from small trinkets to life-size sculptures are created here. Using a variety of tools from hooks and hammers, to saws, chisels and files, the artists turn soapstone, sandstone, marble, and jade into beautiful works of art. On the outskirts of Mamallapuram, the stone carvers place finished pieces, some standing ten feet high and three feet wide behind their work buildings.

AS STRONG AS SILK

By Alana Fickes & Ellen Webber

So much of India's color, richness and diversity is reflected in its textiles. One particular industry involved in creating textiles is silk sari weaving. With modern times, this universally flattering garment is increasingly being woven on mechanized looms with artificial fibers such as polyester, nylon or rayon. Although becoming more and more rare, handloom-woven silk saris are still made today. One such place is a temple in the city of Kumbakonam, where Kamsan Kondal and his family continue hand weaving saris and scarves, as carried down through generations. The saris he and his family produce can take more than 15 days to weave, depending on the intricacy of the design.

IMPRESSION

By Serena Wells

The backwaters that make up much of the district of Alleppey, Kerala, provide unique views of the land-scape and people in every direction.

THE MARKETPLACE

By Joshua J. Anahonak, Courtney Black,
Rebecca Dornewass, Alana Fickes, Sybill Jecker,
Madelynne Nehl, Stephanie Newell & Ellen Webber

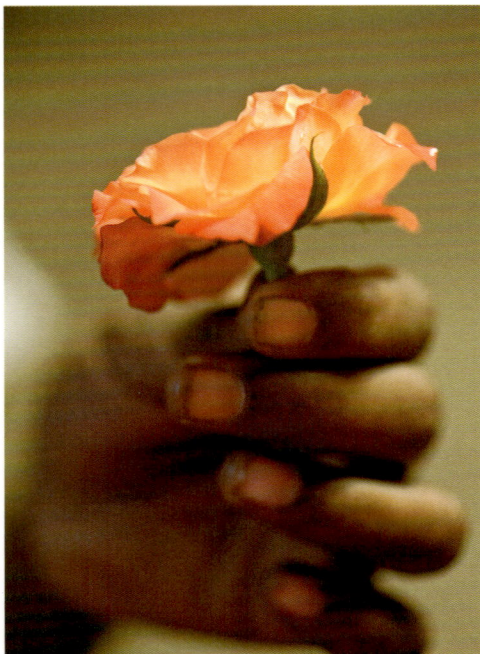

Markets are an essential part of life in the South Indian states of Karnataka, Kerala and Tamil Nadu. The streets bustle with vendors, autos and customers, buying and selling endless goods. Fresh flowers and produce are piled high in baskets and bins, with elaborate displays enticing passing people to stop and peruse the selection. Many markets are open seven days a week and each is unique to the city where it is found.

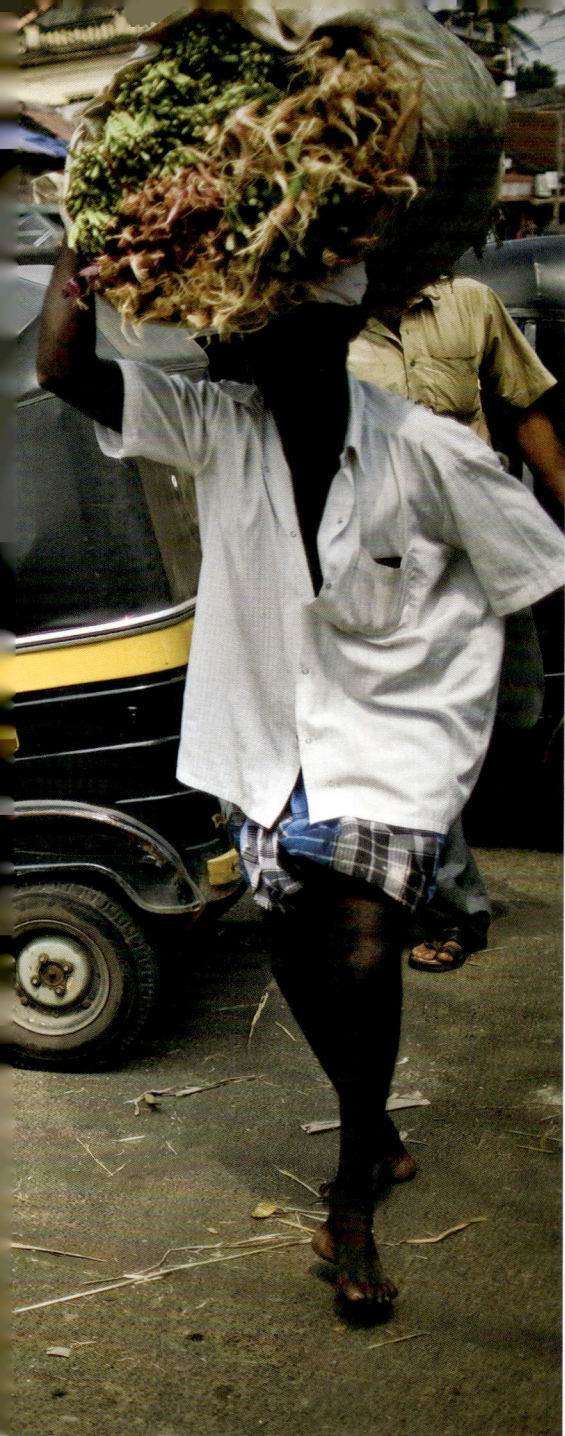

FAITH

By Adam Herrera

Hindu temple cities of South India provide residents and pilgrims alike with a place for meditation, prayer and worship.

CONVICTION

By Jeff Johns

Lavishly decorated participants are a common sight at Hindu processions around temples in Chennai, Tamil Nadu. Festivals are often held in honor of Hindu Gods such as Ganesh, the God of karma and good luck.

DIVINE ALIGNMENT

By Jennifer Homsher

Hinduism is the third largest world religion with 930 million Hindus currently living in India and is often stated as the "oldest living tradition," dating back to 3,000 B.C. Many of its rituals are designed to spark awareness of the divine and receive its blessings. Hindus engage in pujas (cleansings or worship) at their chosen temples or their home altars in order to receive the characteristic blessings of the god to whom they pray.

Various substances are believed to ignite and enlighten the soul through the senses and are incorporated into daily practice. The sensation of bare feet on an ancient temple's granite stones, which are believed to hold and emanate power, helps quicken the soul, for instance, while lighting a camphor lamp sparks the soul with its divine atoms through sight. The aroma of roses, jasmine, and incense arouses one's sense of smell and again, is another source of quickening. Other rituals encourage selflessness to gain alignment, such as feeding the temple catfish, a representation of the deity, which results in good health. And practices such as

making a kollam, or chalk drawing, in front of one's doorway or altar are believed to help women stimulate their minds and concentration, as well as welcome in guests and Lakshmi, the goddess of wealth and prosperity. All of these practices are used to ignite and align the individual with the divine, thereby encouraging the development of the soul, and reducing one's suffering in this world and the next.

ANCIENT ART

By Sybill Jecker, Jeff Johns, Samantha Murphy, Cesare Naldi & Amanda Reyes

Kathakali is a traditional art form of the southern Indian state of Kerala, and dates back centuries. The name Kathakali is derived from the Malayalam words katha, or story, and kali, meaning play.

Actors are traditionally masked in elaborate, hand-painted make-up made from ash and natural plant dyes, and wear lavishly adorned costumes. The performance is set to the beats of various percussion instruments and the stories they recreate are typically ancient Hindu epics, told solely through facial expressions, rhythmic movement and hand gestures, known as mudras. The intricate nature of the show calls for highly skilled performers, many of whom have trained their whole lives to perfect this technique.

Kathakali ensembles are often made up of families and friends who have been performing together for many years. Kathakali can be found throughout the state and is a popular tourist attraction in large cities such as Trivandrum and Cochin.

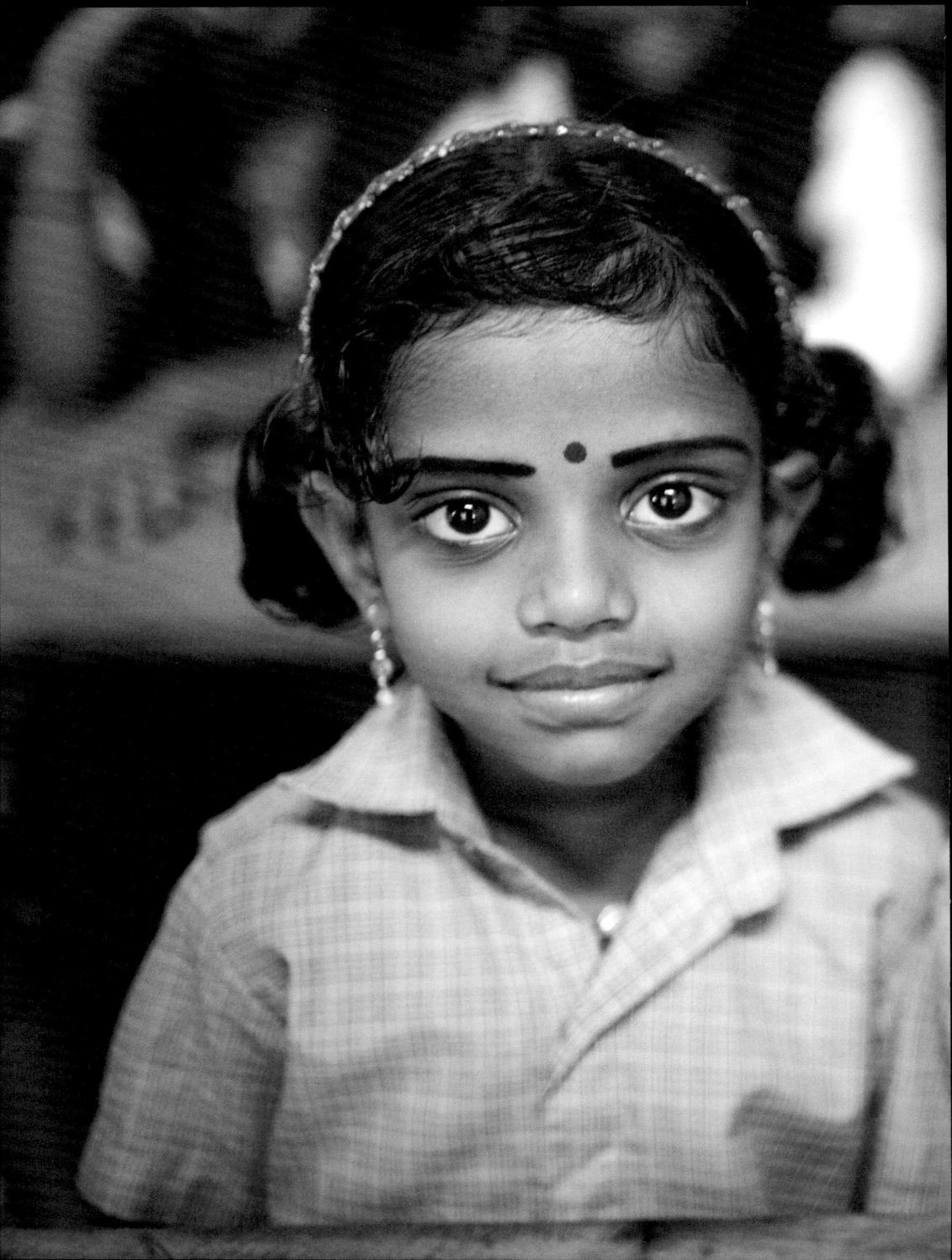

RHYTHM

Photo by Sybill Jecker

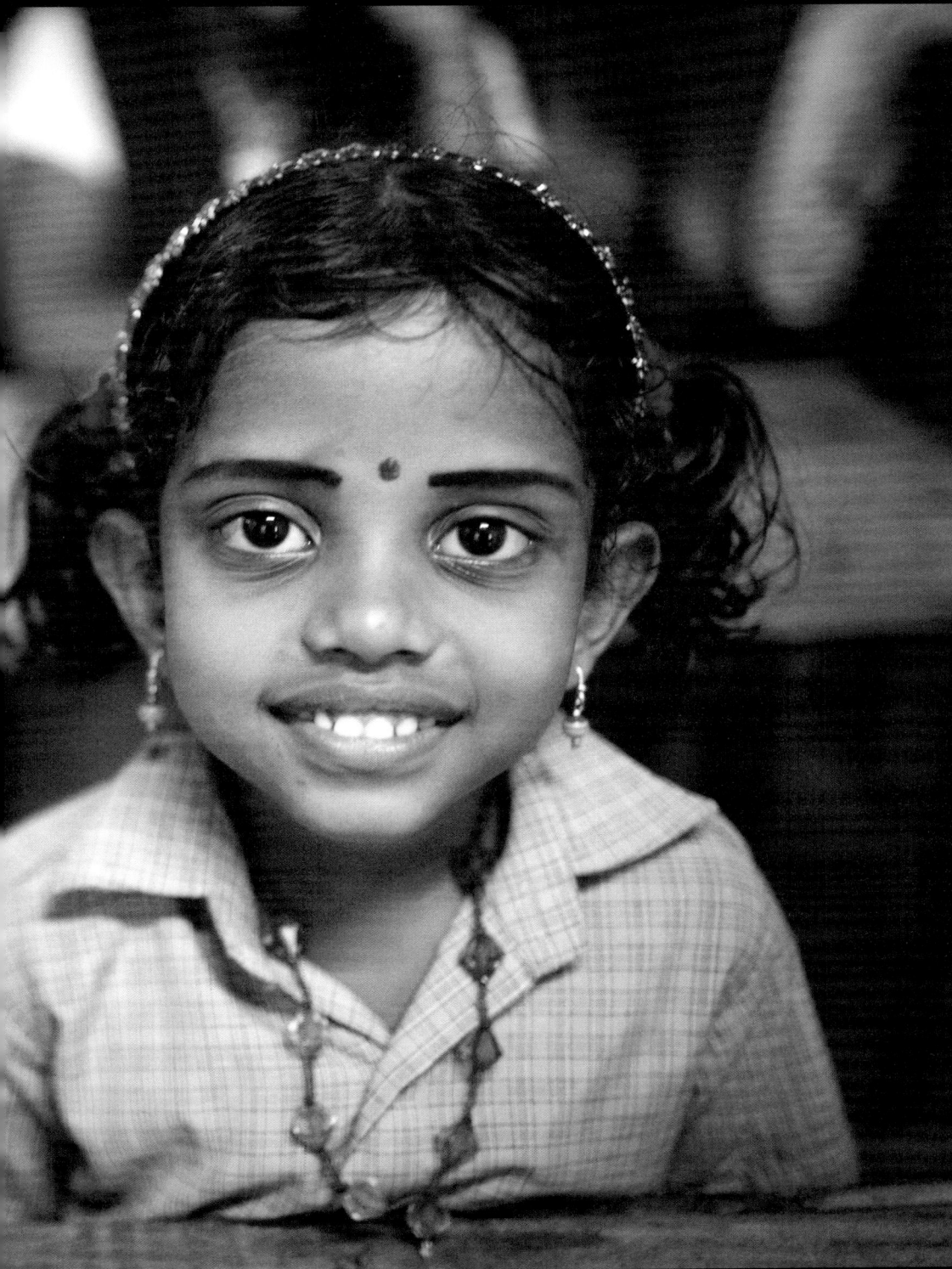

MOVING A NATION

By Beatriz Barragan Horn & Janine Stengel

"Being on the roads is what we do most of our lives. If you talk about chaos or chaos theory it actually works perfectly well in India," says Venkataraaman, member of the Indian Railway Fan Club. Approximately 90% of the Indian population depends on public transportation. The Indian train system is the second largest employer in the world, moving five billion passengers annually and an average of 14 million passengers each day.

The new found wealth of many Indians, however, has enabled them to purchase private vehicles, at the rate of adding 1,200 to 1,400 a day to the flow of traffic in Bangalore. The Indian government's inability to rapidly reconfigure the current infrastructure to one that can accommodate these vehicles, has resulted in mayhem as the rule of the road. The additional vehicles are further impacting the air quality in this region.

Chennai, in contrast, has been able to implement a strong urban and suburban transport system based off of the 1930s British infrastructure, which relied primarily on the use of trains. This urban railway provides greater connectivity to all classes and reduces the need for personal vehicles.

MIND, BODY & SOUL
By Sybill Jecker

Yoga is commonly known as a physical and mental discipline, which originated in India and is practiced by many to achieve good health and inner peace. Schools of yoga can be found all around the world in various forms. The Sivananda Yoga Vedanta Centre, in Kerala's capital of Trivandrum, is nestled among homes in the West Fort area of the city. Here, all levels of yoga practitioners, from beginner to advanced, can attend sessions on a rooftop classroom where the fresh air and rising sun provide a beautiful environment for nourishing the mind, body, and soul.

Founded in 1987 by Swami Vishnudevananda, the center's teachings are based around the 'Five Points of Yoga,' which are basic principles that can be easily followed to create a healthy lifestyle. The Five Points of Yoga are asana (proper exercise), pranayama (proper breathing), savasana (proper relaxation), vegetarian (proper diet) and vedanta and dhyana (proper breathing and meditation.) According to Yoga Schrya Surendran, an instructor at the Centre, implementing these five points can help a person reach a higher state, both mentally and physically.

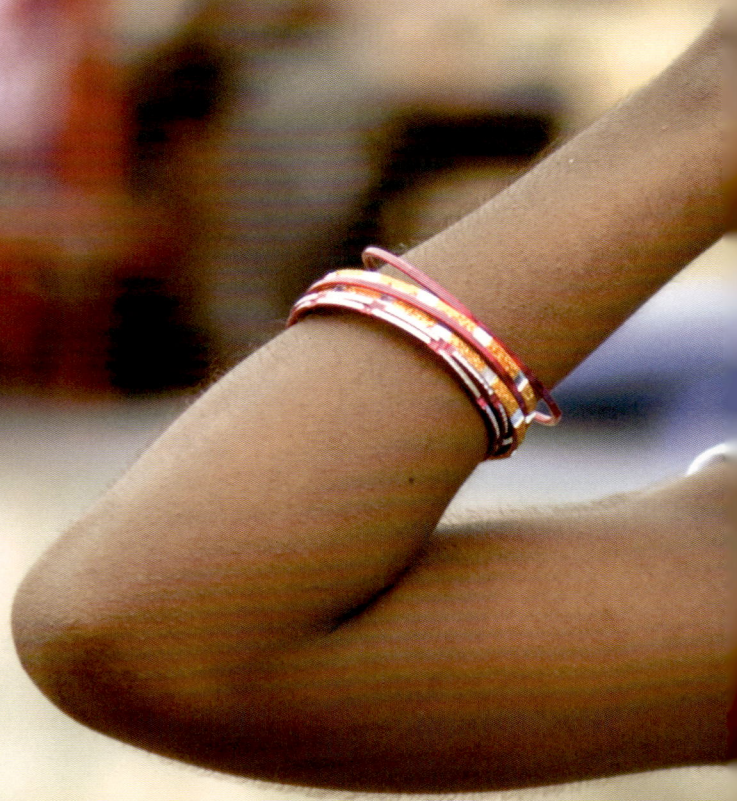

INNOCENCE

By Stephanie Newell

The presence of children is strong throughout the alleyways and streets of Kanyakumari, Tamil Nadu.

SOUND OF THE SOUTH

By Paul Myers & Serena Wells

The indigenous music of South India is called Carnatic and has long been believed to be a gift from the gods. Carnatic music diverged from Northern Hindustani music in the 16th and 17th centuries. In the South, the epicenter for these divine tunes is the Madras Music Academy in Chennai.

The Music Academy was founded in 1928 to promote education and the practice of traditional Indian music. Today, the school hosts several conferences, concerts, and competitions a year and is home to one of the finest collections of rare and historical Indian manuscripts and music books in the world.

Students here can learn to play a variety of instruments from the vina to the violin and mridangam. There is also a Music College at the Academy, where students can pursue a career in music education.

NO BOUNDARIES

By Cesare Naldi

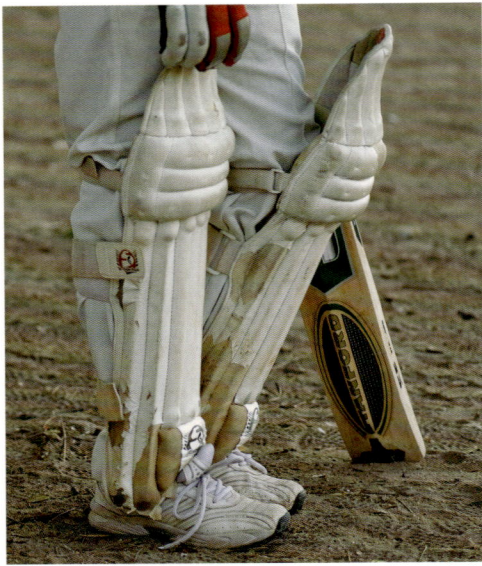

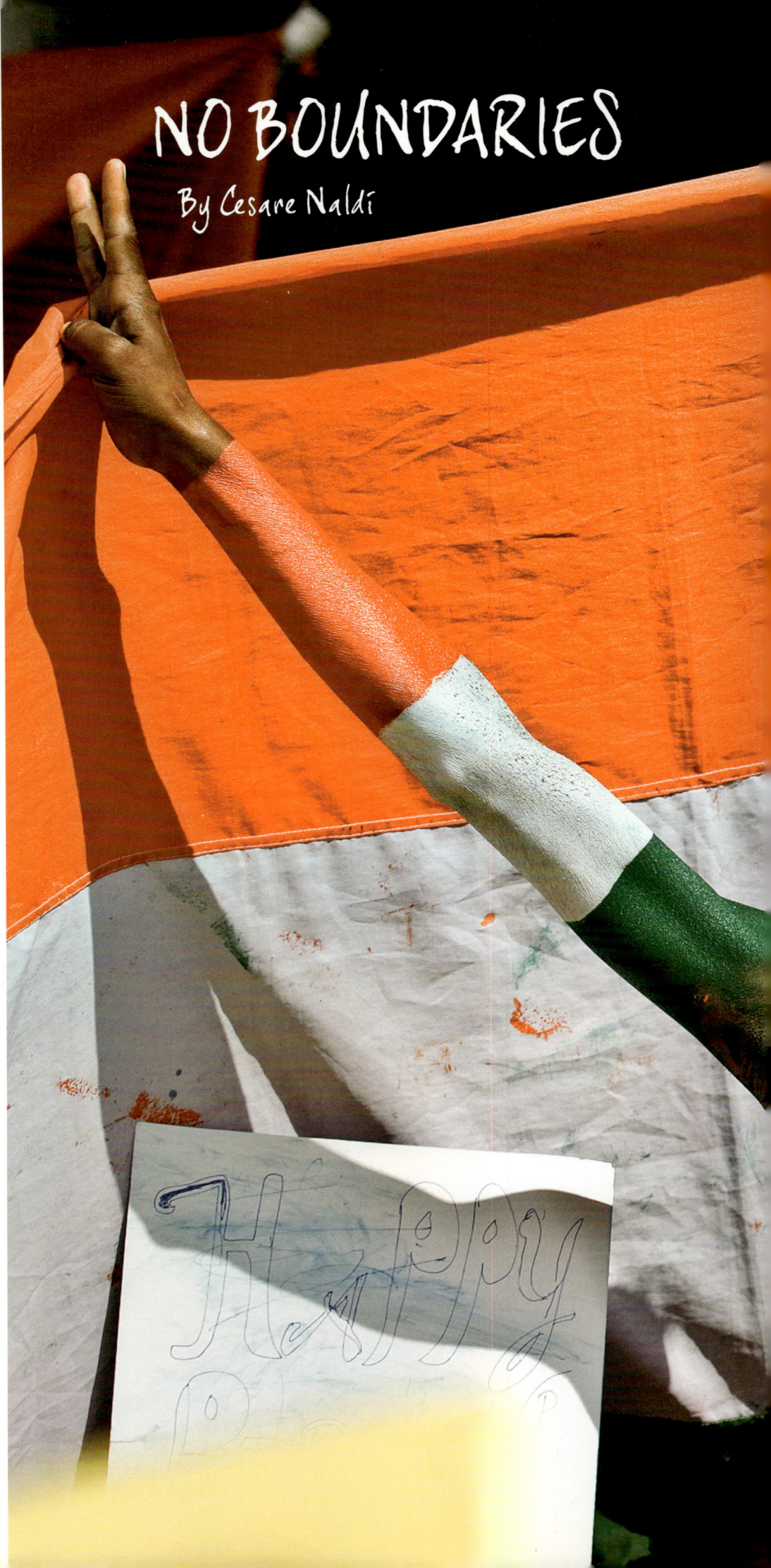

Cricket is the most popular sport in all of India and is played just about anywhere space allows. On holidays and weekends, public spaces fill with cricketers, many of whom are children scarcely taller than the bats they wield. On beachfronts, cricket fields merge one into the other creating an intricate sequence of playgrounds in which players from different games happily mix. The game can be found in parking lots, alleyways, pastures and rice paddies, but perhaps the most popular place to find a game is right outside your door.

In professional and international arenas, cricket matches command huge crowds and a single game can last up to five days. In minor leagues, it is not uncommon for an entire herd of sheep to graze on the field without the slightest interruption of play.

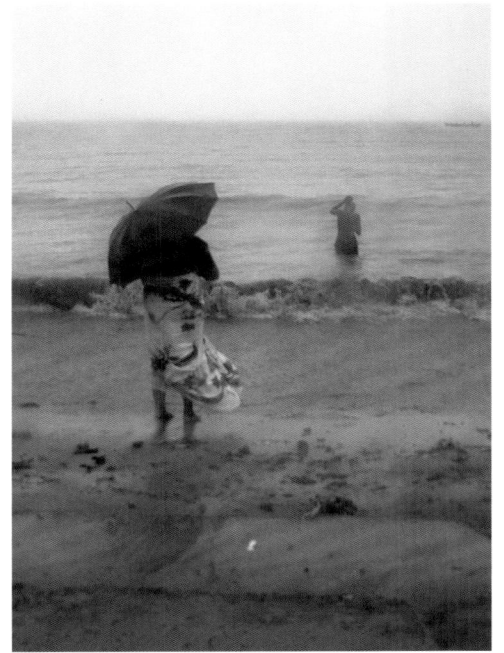

SPACES BETWEEN

By Ellen Webber

In India, at least in the south, there are some rules. They are mostly unspoken rules, the kind that somehow seamlessly weave their way into the fabric of lives. There is the rule that the wife must follow paces behind the husband when walking down the street. A married woman should not be seen running around town with single friends, or after dark without her husband. The few times couples can be seen touching is when a woman, riding side-saddle and sari-clad on the back of a motorcycle, clings to the man driving. Teenage boys are permitted to be openly affectionate amongst themselves, while girls must maintain a reserved decorum.

In India, the spaces between male and female, public and private, can be seen.

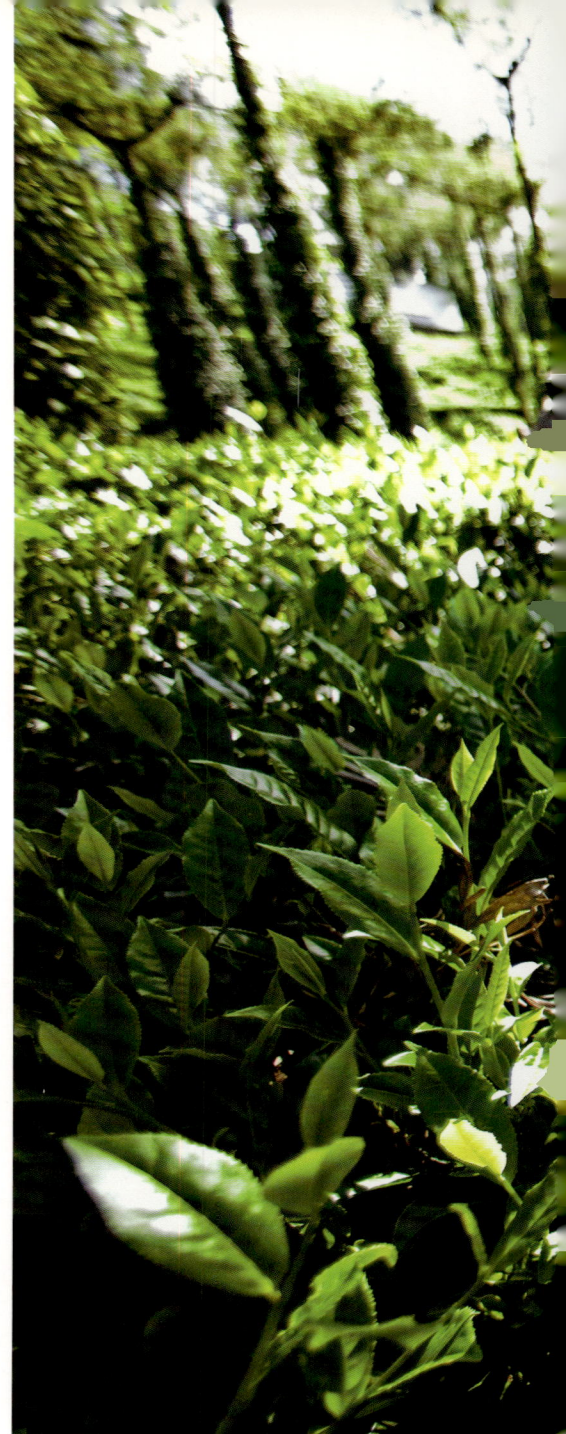

FROM THE EARTH

By Joshua J. Anahonak, Cesare Naldi, Madelynne Nehl & Nicole Vinisky

Tea is a vital tradition and commodity in India, having earned India large annual revenues. The climate of South India allows tea to flourish year round where it is largely grown in the mountainous regions of the Western Ghats in the states of Kerala and Tamil Nadu. The majority of tea plantation workers live with their families on the grounds. Women often work in the fields while the men work in the factories.

The cultivation of tea plants is the foundation of this industry. The process begins with small plastic bags of sand and dirt used to grow new tea shoots. Once filled, the bags will spend three months growing uncovered, then three months covered in plastic to create a green house effect, and finally six months in a field before being transferred to the estate to mature for picking. Once picked, the leaves are weighed and

left in a trough for 12 to 14 hours for physical and chemical withering, which contributes to the tea's final color. The tea is then sorted by leaf size into the different grades of loose and powdered teas.

Tea is a major staple in the Indian diet. It is commonly blended with milk, sweetener and spices into a beverage commonly known as chai.

IMAGINATION

By Ellen Webber

Driving through town on a rainy day, the water
streaming down a window swirls the colors of
South India.

SILVER SCREEN OF CHENNAI

By Jennifer Homsher

In the United States they call it Hollywood, in Mumbai, India its referred to as Bollywood, and in Chennai its known as Kollywood. Regardless of the location, these three words mean the same thing

to the people that use them—motion pictures.

For years Bollywood has been considered India's motion picture epicenter, but recently Kollywood

films have become increasingly popular in India and neighboring countries such as Sri Lanka, Singapore, and Malaysia, and Kollywood is quickly gaining a reputation as one of India's leading

entertainment resources.

In *Leelai*, a romantic comedy and the first major film by Director Andrew Louis, two information technology workers in Chennai fall in love over the phone. As with most Tamil films, singing and dancing play a major role in the movie and are a primary focus during filming. However, some Indian actors are finding it difficult to make the transition from Bollywood to Kollywood.

Bollywood is located in the south-central state of Karnataka, where the primary native language is Hindi. However, the recently booming industry of Kollywood is located in the south-eastern state of Tamil Nadu, where the local native language is Tamil. The two locations are separated by only a few hundred miles, but many actors choosing to participate in Kollywood films are discovering they need to learn to speak and sing in Tamil first.

Manasi Parehk is one such actress. Manasi, an English and Hindi speaking actress from Mumbai, was forced to spend several months studying her lines and songs in Tamil to prepare her for her lead role in *Leelai*, a language she was completely unfamiliar with prior to filming. The film was released in Chennai on February 14, 2009.

Elections '08

WATCHING WITH HOPE

By Adam Herrera, Jeff Johns, Samantha Murphy, Paul Myers & Amanda Reyes

On Wednesday, November 5, 2008 at 9:00 a.m., local time, Senator Barack Obama announced his victory over Senator John McCain in the United States Presidential Election, and his victory was greeted with resounding applause in Chennai, Tamil Nadu. Over 300 people attended the 2008 U.S. Presidential Elections – Open House at the Taj Commoral Hotel sponsored by the U.S. Consulate General in Chennai.

Members of the local press, school children, U.S. citizens living in India, as well as tourists, attended the event. Activities included taking photos with cardboard cutouts of the candidates, discussion of the Indian American involvement in the political process, and mock election booths to vote for your favorite candidate.

Once the results were in, inquisitive high school and college students, along with foreigners, discussed the impact of the election results on Indo-U.S. relations while drinking tea together.

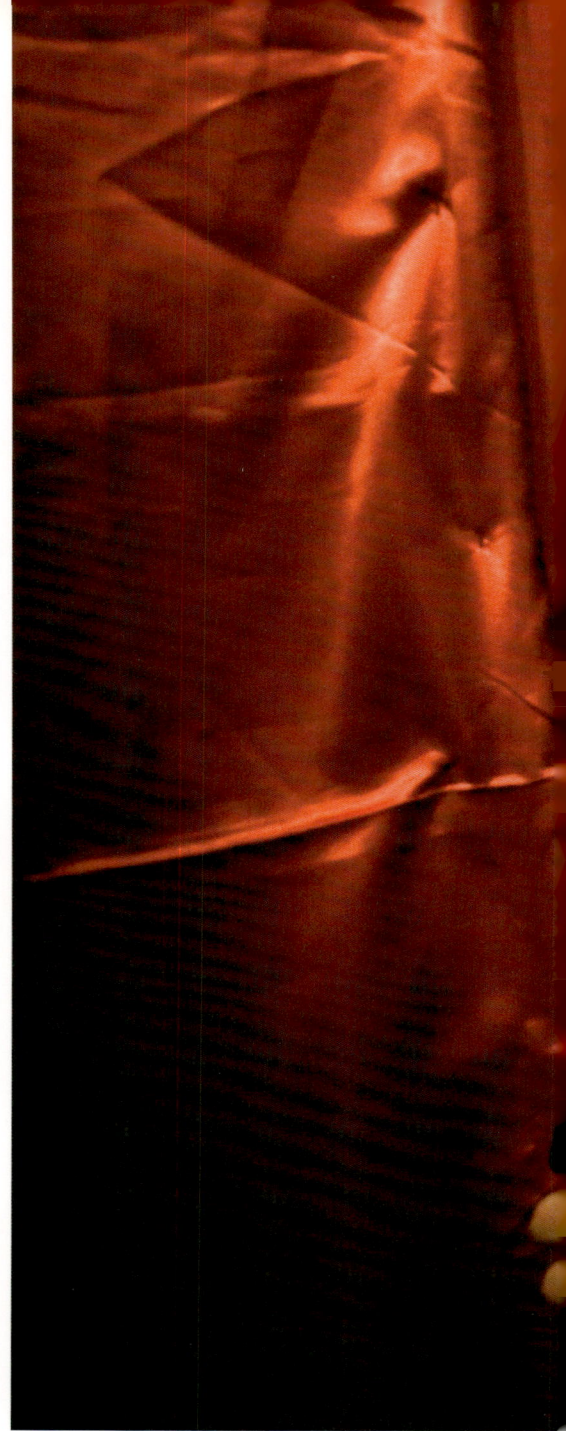

CHARACTER

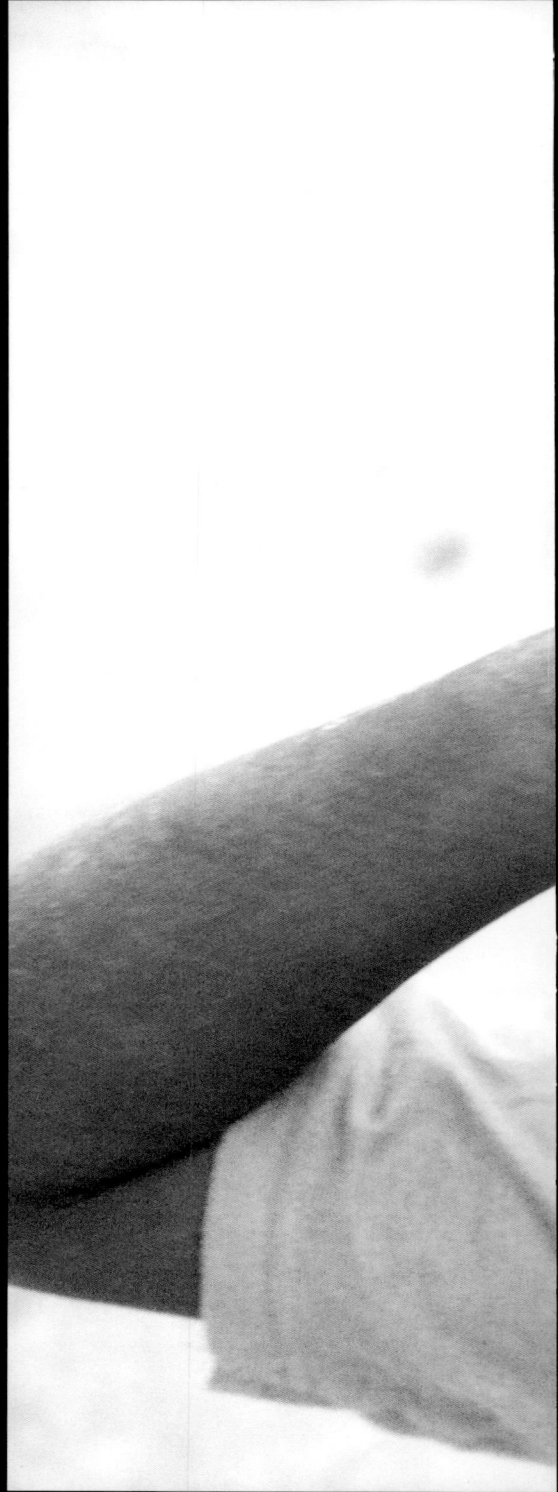

Photo by Courtney Black

QUICK FIX

By Paul Myers

Need your fountain pen fixed? A new battery in your calculator or camera? Your lighter refilled with lighter fluid? None of these tasks is too small for Pazhani A. at the Pen Hospital.

A small shop located near Ayurveda College in Trivandrum, Kerala, the Pen Hospital prolongs the life of many small household items, though Pazhani A.'s specialty is fixing lighters. Open for 60 years, Pazhani A. took over the family business 15 years ago from his father.

Pazhani A. has a steady stream of customers and neighbors who stop by his shop throughout the day. He keeps matchboxes filled with different sized crystals and batteries, to fit all presented items, and checks them for fit, one by one.

EN HOSPITAL

BEAUTY
By Nicole Vinisky

Specialty markets selling everything from flowers to fish can be found in most towns. Flowers are often worn in a woman's hair or used for religious ceremonies throughout South India.

LOVE OF DANCE

By Amanda Reyes

Dancing since age four, Minal Prabu, now 51, takes great pride in being a dance instructor in Bangalore, Karnataka. Minal brings her passion for dancing into her work and for the past 32 years, she has enjoyed passing this knowledge on to the next generation of dancers.

Her students range in age from seven to 45 years old and are taught the Indian dance of Bharatanatyam, one of India's classical dance forms. It is an art that blends dance and music with a focus on the body, mind and soul. The classes include warm-ups based on yoga, along with exercises in Nritta (pure dance) and Abhinaya (expression). Technical details regarding rhythm and music for Bharatanatyam are also explored. Minal teaches at three different locations each day, ranging from a formal studio to a room in her apartment's garage.

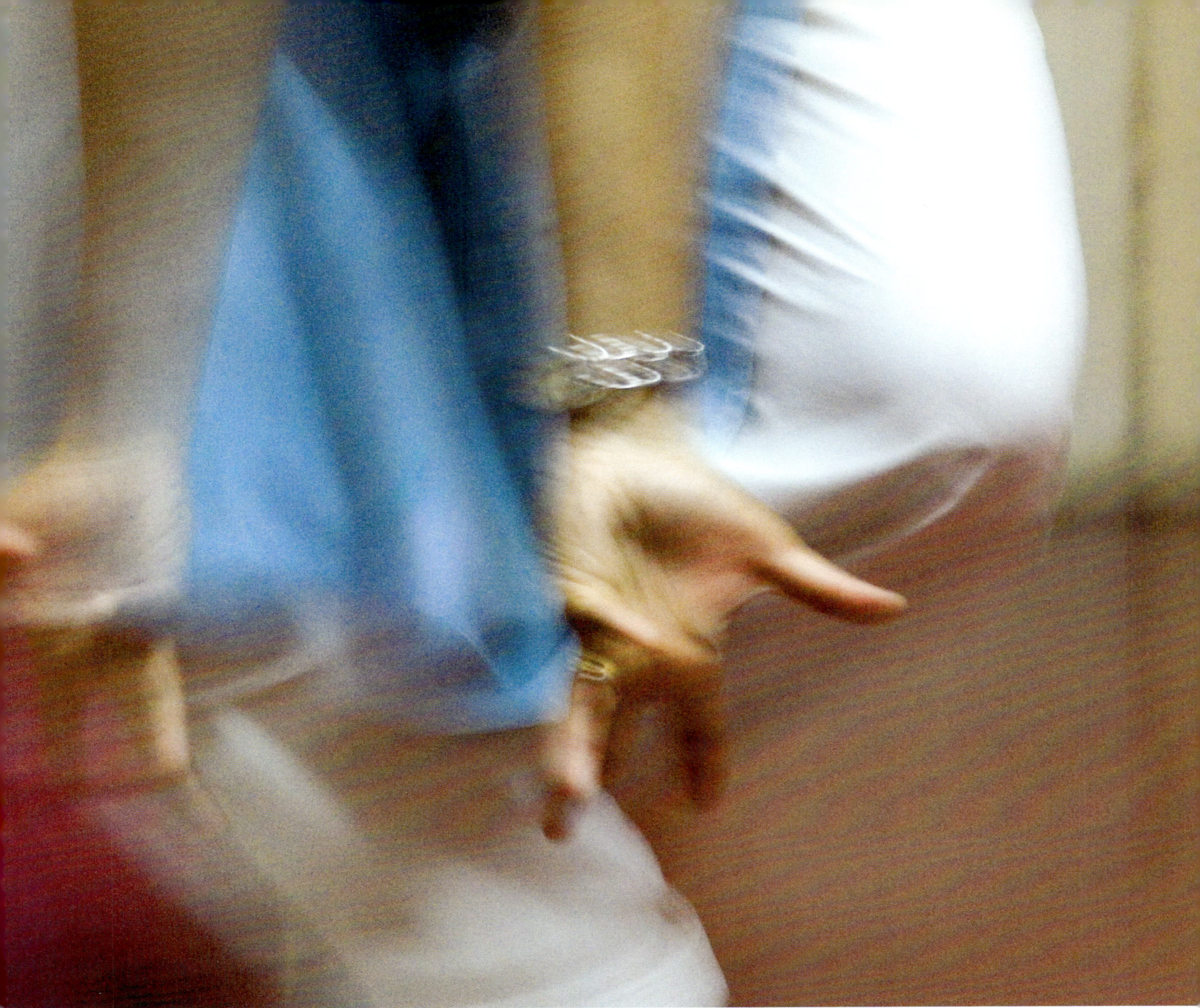

PEACE

By Jennifer Homsher

The quiet comfort of meditation, whether attained sitting on a temple floor or playing outside with a string of jasmine flowers, brings tranquility to those who seek it.

The bond between a mahout and his elephant is powerful. Mahout is the term used for the caretaker and trainer of an elephant, and in Kerala, most captive elephants are owned by individual families or a temple trust. Since elephants can live to be anywhere from 60 to 90 years old, most elephants are passed down from one generation to the next with a single mahout often spending his whole life with a single animal.

There are more than 1,200 trained elephants in captivity and around 5,200 wild elephants in Kerala. They are an essential part of Keralan life and are used for temple ceremonies, as well as in the timber industry throughout South India.

Elephants require an incredible amount of exercise to stay healthy, so during the rainy season when work is slow, many mahouts employ their elephants in the tourist industry to supplement the loss in income and keep the elephant fit. It costs about Rs 3,000 or $60 a day to care for an elephant, and these photographed elephants work at Tusker Trail Elephant Rides in Kumily, Kerala.

Keralan elephants are typically taller than average Indian elephants, standing at an impressive 12.5 feet, and, prized for their dark colored skin, are considered more beautiful than other species of Indian elephants. White elephants are prized even more still, and are often chosen for religious ceremonies. Elephants slowly turn white while in captivity due to daily bathing where the mahout scrubs the elephant's entire body with coconut husks and stones.

TUSKER TRAIL

By Rebecca Dornewass, Madelynne Nehl & Nicole Vinisky

A UNIVERSAL CITY

By Stephanie Newell

Auroville, located in the state of Tamil Nadu, is a township dedicated to human unity through diversity and sustainable living. Chali Grinnell, a 42-year-old American, has lived in Auroville for over half her life. She spent her childhood in Auroville during its early years, moving there shortly after it started in 1968. During this time, Auroville lacked any kind of formal education system for its residents, so in order to receive a structured education, Chali had to attend boarding school at Kodaikanal International School. Later, Chali returned to the United States to earn her high school and college degrees.

After working for a few years in the US, Chali returned to Auroville to raise a family of her own. Wanting her children to have the opportunity to receive a more traditional education in Auroville, Chali founded 'Future School' with fellow Aurovillian, Luk Gastmans.

Future School is a high school that was modeled around the British school system. Chali currently teaches ninth and tenth grade English and biology at Future School and lives in Auroville with her husband and two sons.

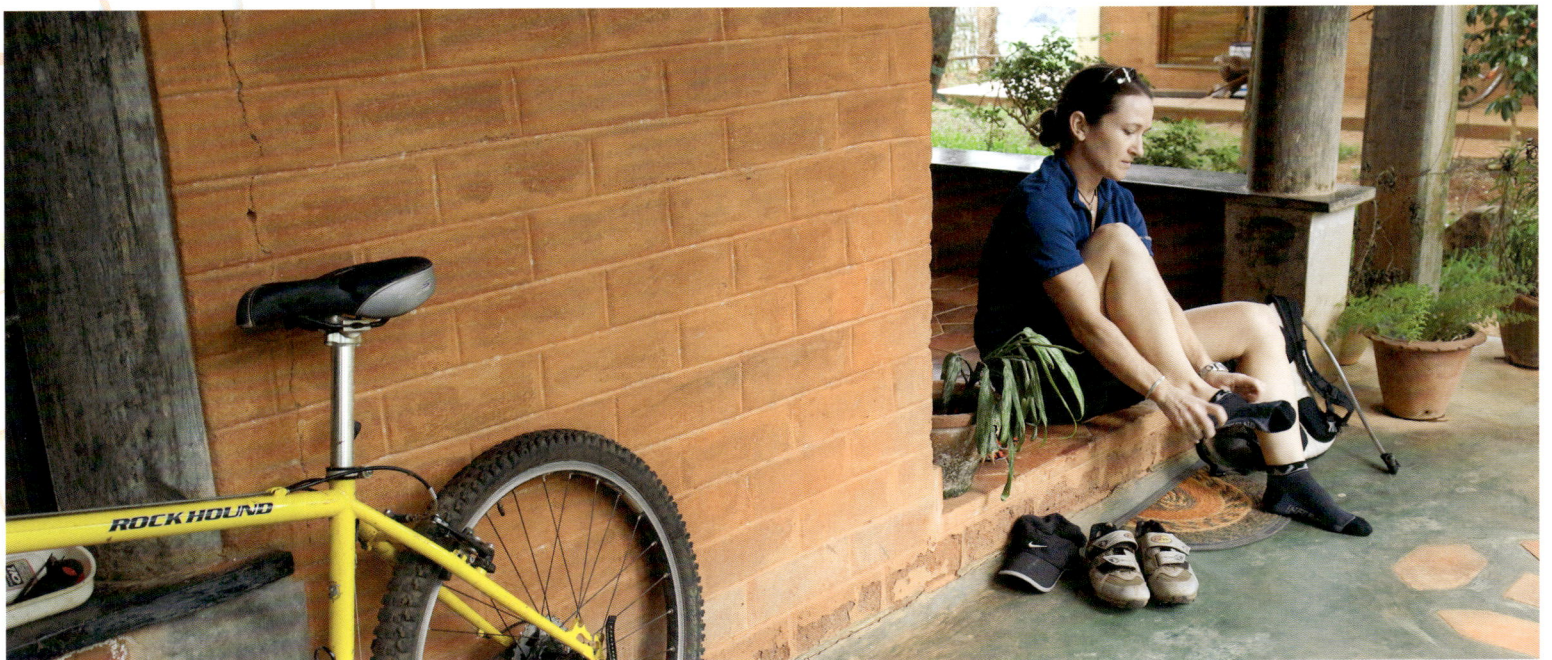

CULTURE

By Madelynne Nehl

The Devaraja Market in Mysore, Karnataka, is filled with many small shops selling a variety of goods, but is best known for the sale of colorful kumkum powders.

HEALING SPIRIT
By Sybill Jecker

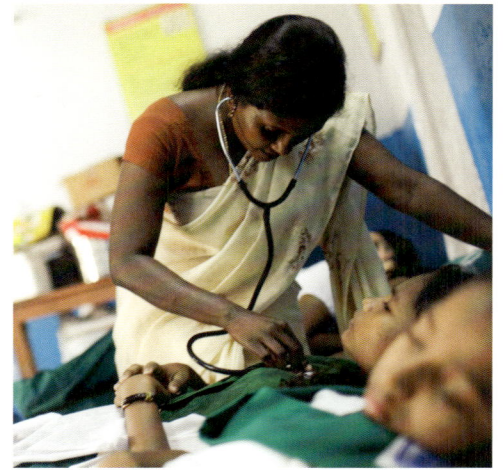

At Government Girls Higher Secondary School Cotton Hill in Trivandrum, Kerala, Dr. Rani Kamalan provides medical care and motherly advice for the 5,700 female students, as well as the faculty and staff, through a small clinic established on the campus. Each day, students line up to see Dr. Rani for various ailments from headaches and dizziness, to injuries and muscle pains. Every patient receives a prescription or a vitamin at the end of her visit. Throughout the day, Dr. Rani also provides intimate group lessons about female issues, including puberty and relationships.

A petite woman at 4' 8", Dr. Rani is, nonetheless, a commanding presence and provides the teenage girls with guidance, and brutal honesty when necessary, to prepare them for the trials of adulthood. Students can be seen by the dozens crowding around the wall where she posts answers to anonymous questions about private matters on life and love. Dr. Rani believes in preventative medicine and feels passionately about teaching the girls how to be healthy now so that they can avoid illnesses in the future.

Most mornings, before entering her clinic around 9:30 a.m., Dr. Rani has already attended a yoga class and had a private English lesson to improve her already impressive vocabulary and grammar. An avid gardener, who lives with her dog, Mabel, Dr. Rani finds happiness in helping her family, friends and students improve their health and find their own way.

ALL IS LOVE

By Serena Wells

Swami Sunildas, a powerful, spiritual Guru who lives in an ashram in Muthalamada, Kerala, has a motto he has been teaching to others since he was a small boy: All is Love.

Sunildas has lived in Muthalamada, widely considered one of the poorest areas in all of Kerala, his entire life, and still lives in his childhood home with his mother and father. As a young boy, Sunildas would use the money he earned at a bank to feed the poor and he would walk to local villages with doctors to help provide care to the needy.

Recently, Sunildas created the The Muthalamada Sneham Charitible Trust, which helps fund several different organizations throughout the Panchayats, a group of nine villages in Muthalamada. The Trust currently supports a free 15-bed hospital, a free ayurvedic medical clinic, a school, and a sewing center, among other services. Surgeries in the Panchayats are almost always arranged free of charge thanks to Sunildas, and his donations to local schools have been substantial over the years including the recent donation of several new computers.

Sunildas has healed many people from all walks of life and is constantly taking people in from the hospital and giving them work and a place to live. He even helped arrange a marriage between two villagers suffering from AIDS so that they may lead more fulfilling lives. He then helped the couple adopt four children – three of whom are also suffering from the disease.

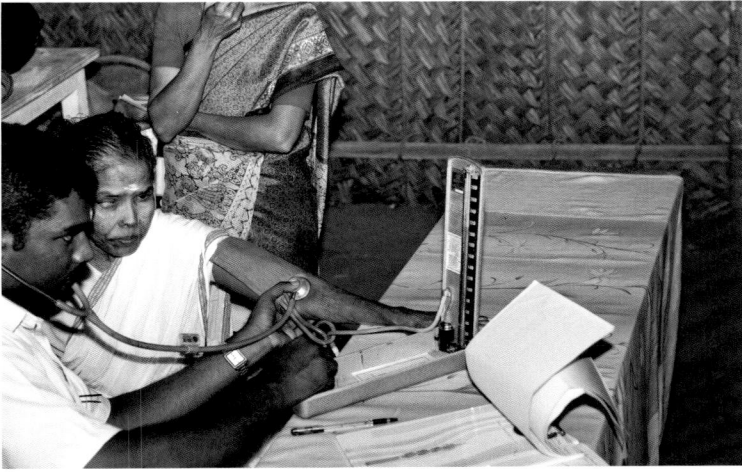

97

RESOLVE

SAVING WILD INDIA

By Adam Herrera

Deep in the jungles of Kerala, a concrete building houses a group of 15 hand-selected students to study wildlife conservation. Every two years, the Indian government in partnership with the Wildlife Conservation Society: India, and the Centre for Wildlife Studies, offers the opportunity for passionate young conservationists to earn their Master's degree in Wildlife Biology and Conservation.
The students come from a variety of backgrounds, many of them having left successful careers in medicine, computer science, and engineering to pursue their passion for conservation.

"India has the second largest human population, and India has the

largest elephant and tiger populations in the world, so there is major conflict between people on one side and conservation on the other," says Dr. Ajith Kumar, an instructor in the program.

Students learn a variety of subjects including entomology, ichthyology, and herpetology from some of the most renowned biologists and conservationists in India. Field research is an essential part of the education process. Students spend weeks in harsh conditions catching frogs, netting fish, and attracting moths with floodlights, for instance, to gain valuable experience.

The jungle is home to a variety of pests and predators that must be contended with on a daily basis, including the constant onslaught of mosquitoes, ticks and leeches and chance encounters with tigers, leopards, and elephants. Leeches are especially troublesome, and can be found by the thousands clinging to undergrowth.

Graduates of the conservation program are among the top in the world. Following the first year of the program, 13 of the 15 students had their dissertations published, a feat that had been unprecedented anywhere else in the world.

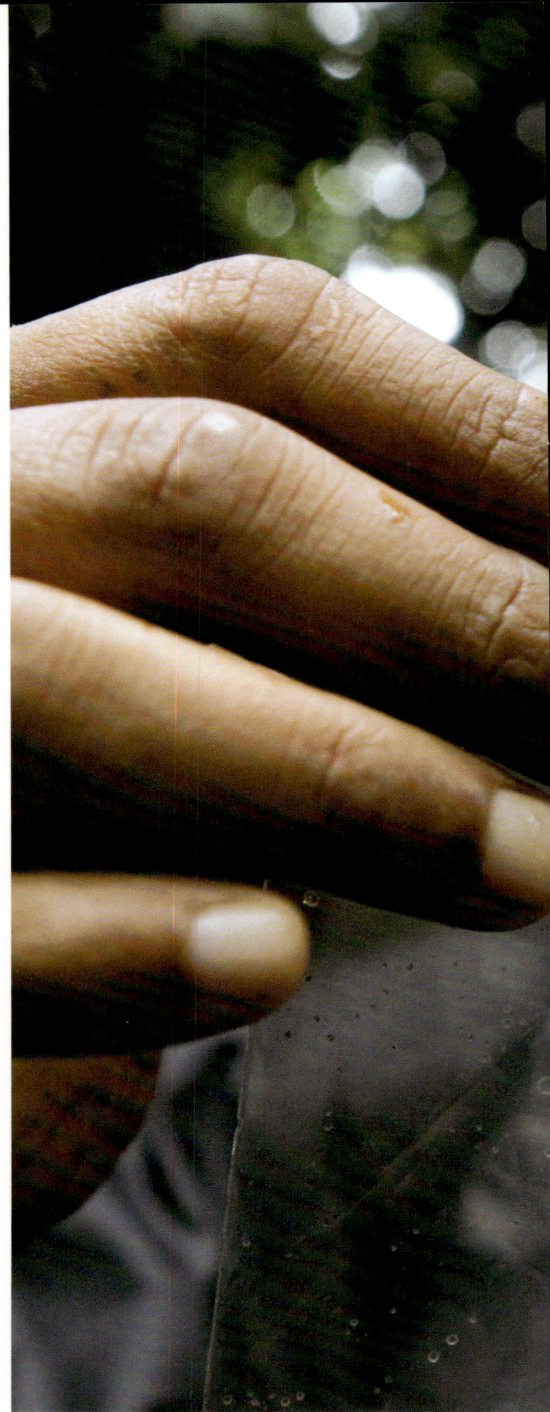

WASTE FOR A LIVING
By Beatriz Barragan Horn & Janine Stengel

In urban India, there are entire families whose livelihood depend on "picking rag," scavenging through piles of trash on the streets, in dumps, and in disease infested urban waterways. Collecting these valuable plastics and cardboards earns them $1 a day. Rag pickers separate the trash they collect and sell it to collection points where it is transferred to a recycler and reincorporated back into the system.

"We have labor, we have manpower," says Vijaja Shenoy from Saahas. Saahas is a non-governmental organization that tries to find solutions related to waste management in Bangalore. "Our consumption of disposable products is not as high [as in the West], but still, the packaging industry is flourishing, so we need to do something about it."

According to Wilma Rodriguez, a director at Saahas, it is due to this waste cycle that Bangalore is able to recycle almost all of its post-consumer materials. In comparison, California recycles only 5% of its post-consumer plastics. Rodriguez says, "The cities have grown too much... the feeling of conveniences have penetrated into our psyche as well...especially with the younger generation who have seen so much of money and who are so rash in their thinking, in their attitudes, and their indifference, so hopefully now...there will be a kind of reversal in this consumerist way of thinking."

105

SIMPLICITY

By Paul Myers

Religious and cultural expectations make shoes an optional accessory throughout this tropical region.

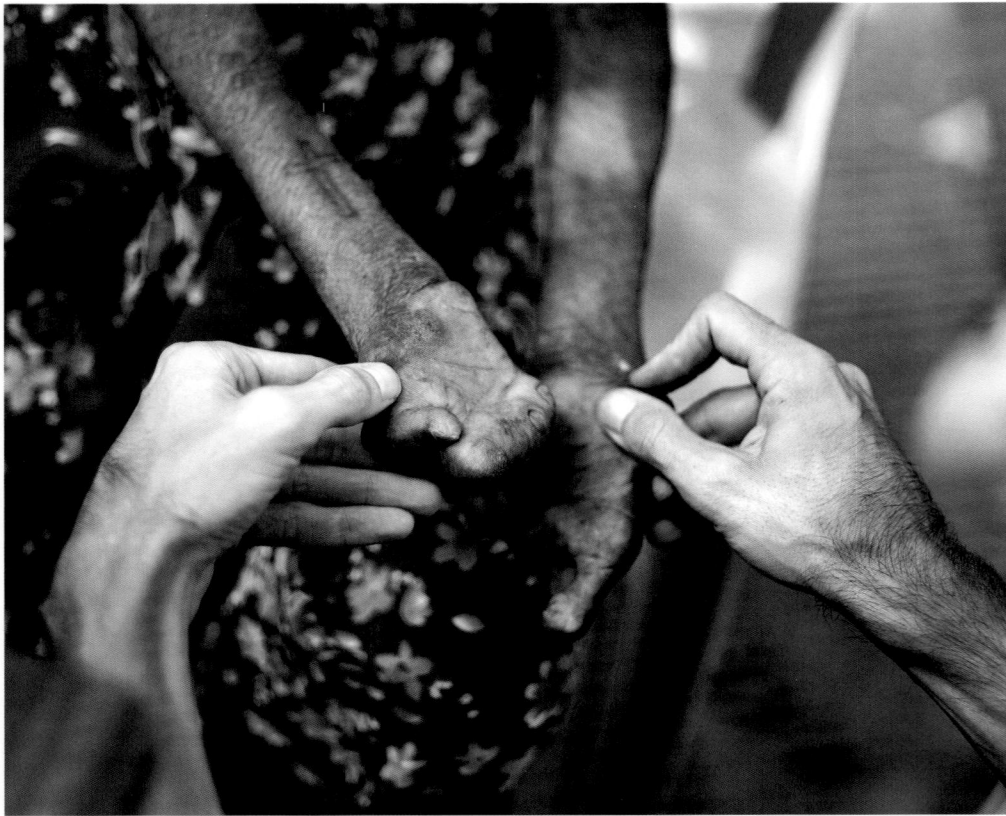

SAVING GRACE

By Courtney Black & Jeff Johns

Leprosy, also referred to as Hanson's disease, is one of the world's oldest documented diseases. It was first recognized in 600 B.C., and has mostly affected the countries we now call Egypt, China and India.

If untreated, leprosy can cause severe damage to the skin, nerves, limbs and eyes, but if caught early enough, leprosy can be stopped in its tracks. Each year, 64% of new leprosy cases worldwide are recorded in India. Many Indians consider leprosy as the worst disease a person can contract, which has resulted in affected people often being pushed to the outskirts of society to live in colonies with other lepers. Some believe that the disease is punishment for something done in a previous life. This social stigma has resulted in thousands of affected people being banned from public schools, as well as being denied public health care in India. Since the mid-1990s, the Indian government has been trying to integrate leprosy care and treatment into most of its health care facilities.

Rising Star Outreach (RSO) is located about two hours outside of the bustling southern Indian city of Chennai and houses hundreds of children whose parents or family members have leprosy. RSO offers a structured school environment, as well as other activities to provide these children with the same opportunities in life as unaffected people. RSO also sponsors a Mobile Medical Unit which heads out weekly to visit leper colonies in the surrounding area. Doctors Senthil Kumar and Karl Kirby donate their time and medical skills to help these patients in any way they can, whether it is through routine medical check-ups, cleaning and bandaging open ulcers, handing out medication for leprosy and other ailments, or transportation to and from the nearest medical clinics.

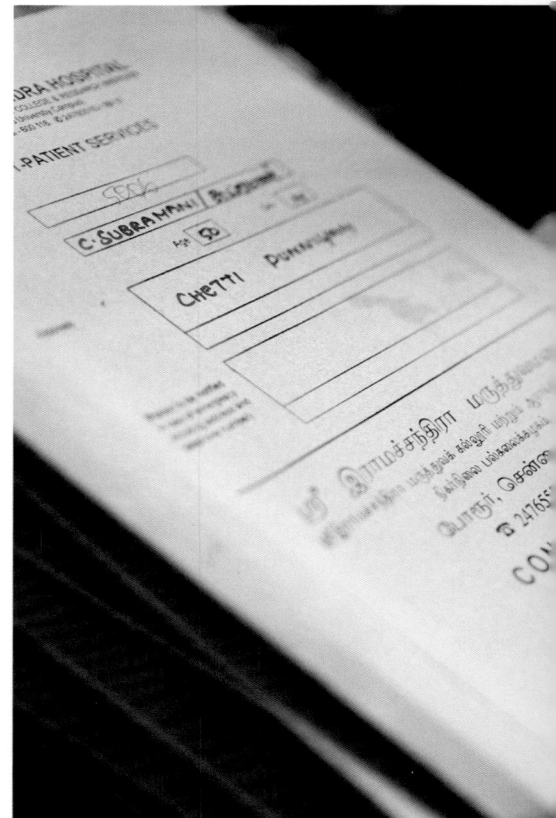

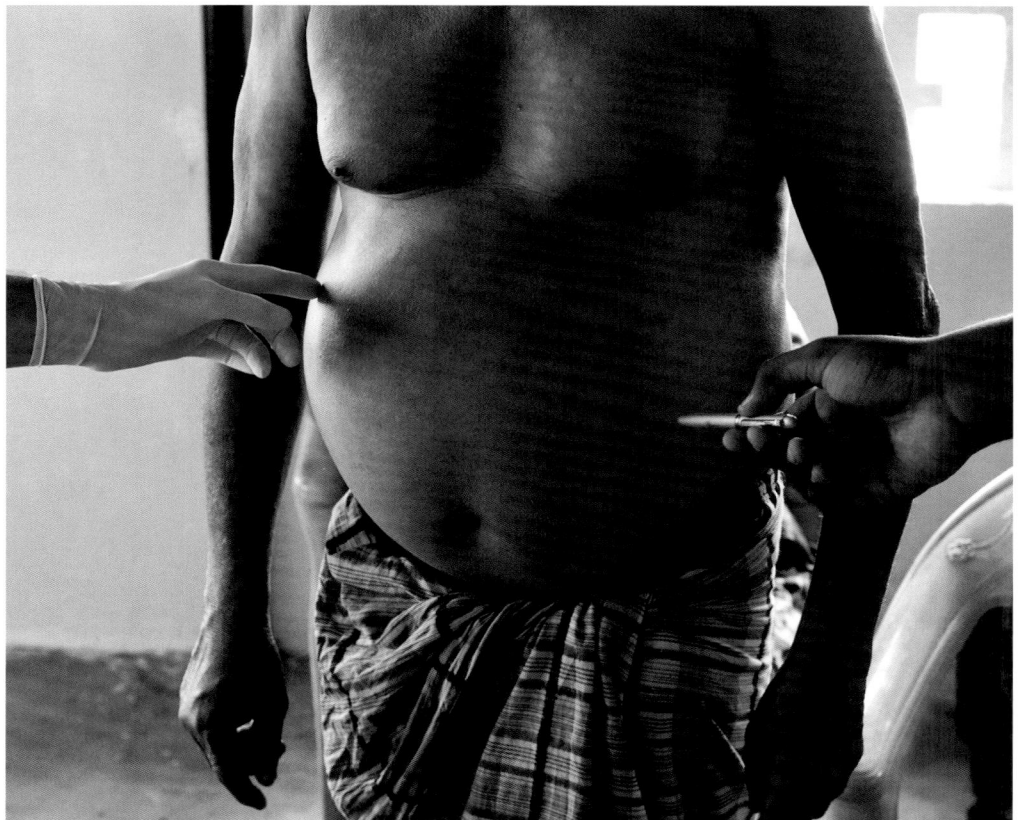

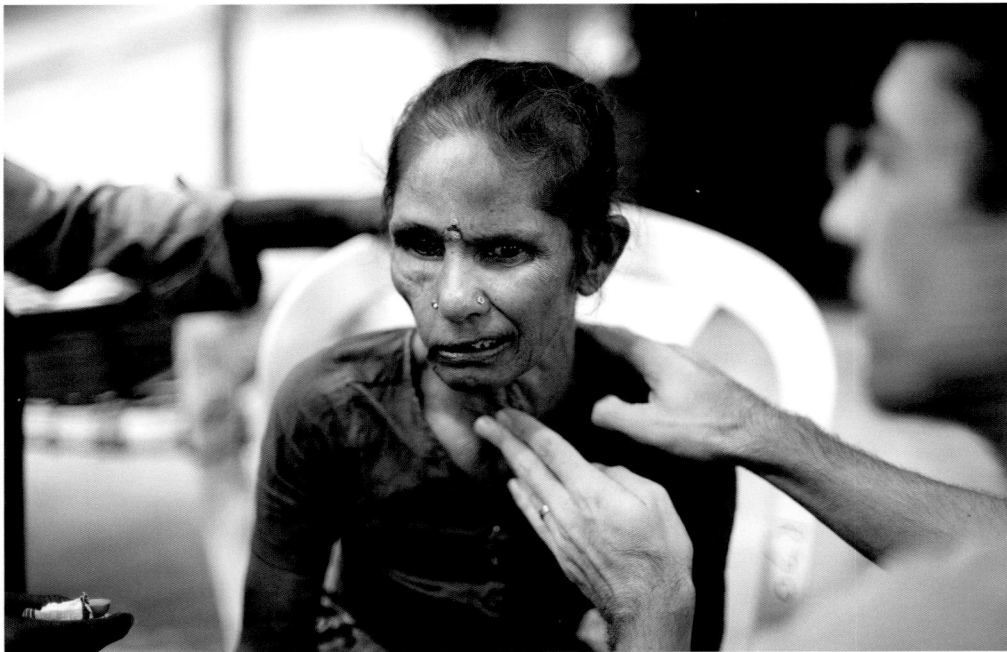

STRENGTH

By Amanda Reyes

Historically, women have maintained a domestic role in Indian society, but recently many have begun to pursue jobs traditionally held by men including law enforcement, health care and engineering positions.

MODERN MARTYR

By Mia Shimabuku

Raja Thomas is a medical rehabilitator for destitute and dying people of Bangalore at New Ark Mission of India: Home of Hope. New Ark, a Christian-based non-profit organization, is funded entirely by donations from local businesses. Currently, Raja and his family live with and care for more than 300 people suffering from a variety of medical issues including AIDS, cancer, and leprosy.

Recently, Raja was arrested by police and beaten while in custody,

events that he claims are a direct result of his belief in Christianity. Raja says that he and his family are under constant assault, receiving death threats and being persecuted for their beliefs. Despite this, members of the community bring new people in need of help to Raja's home weekly. Living amongst the rescued, Raja has made it his life's mission to continue his efforts without any fear for his and his family's lives, standing strong in what he believes in and his purpose.

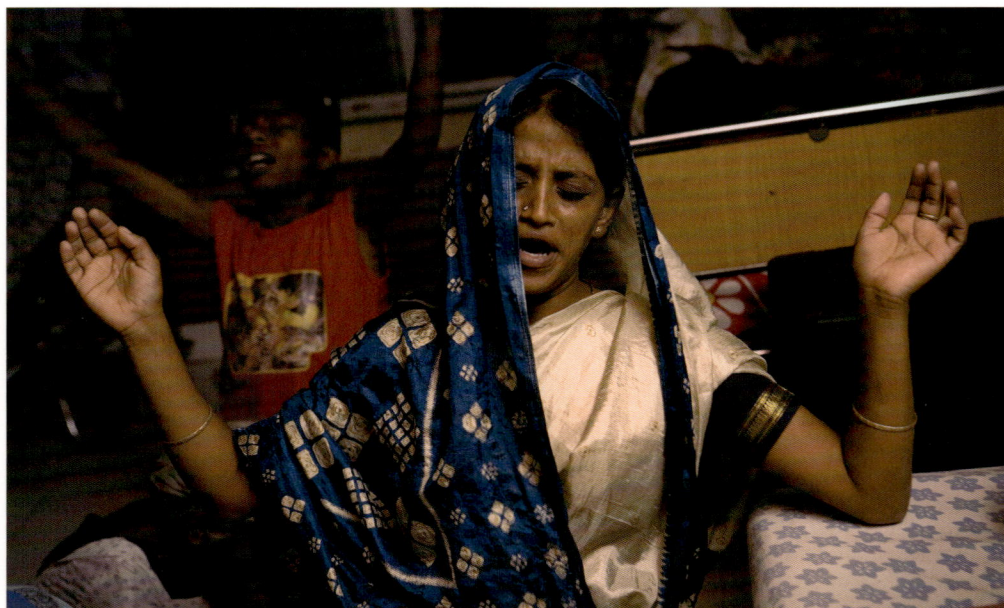

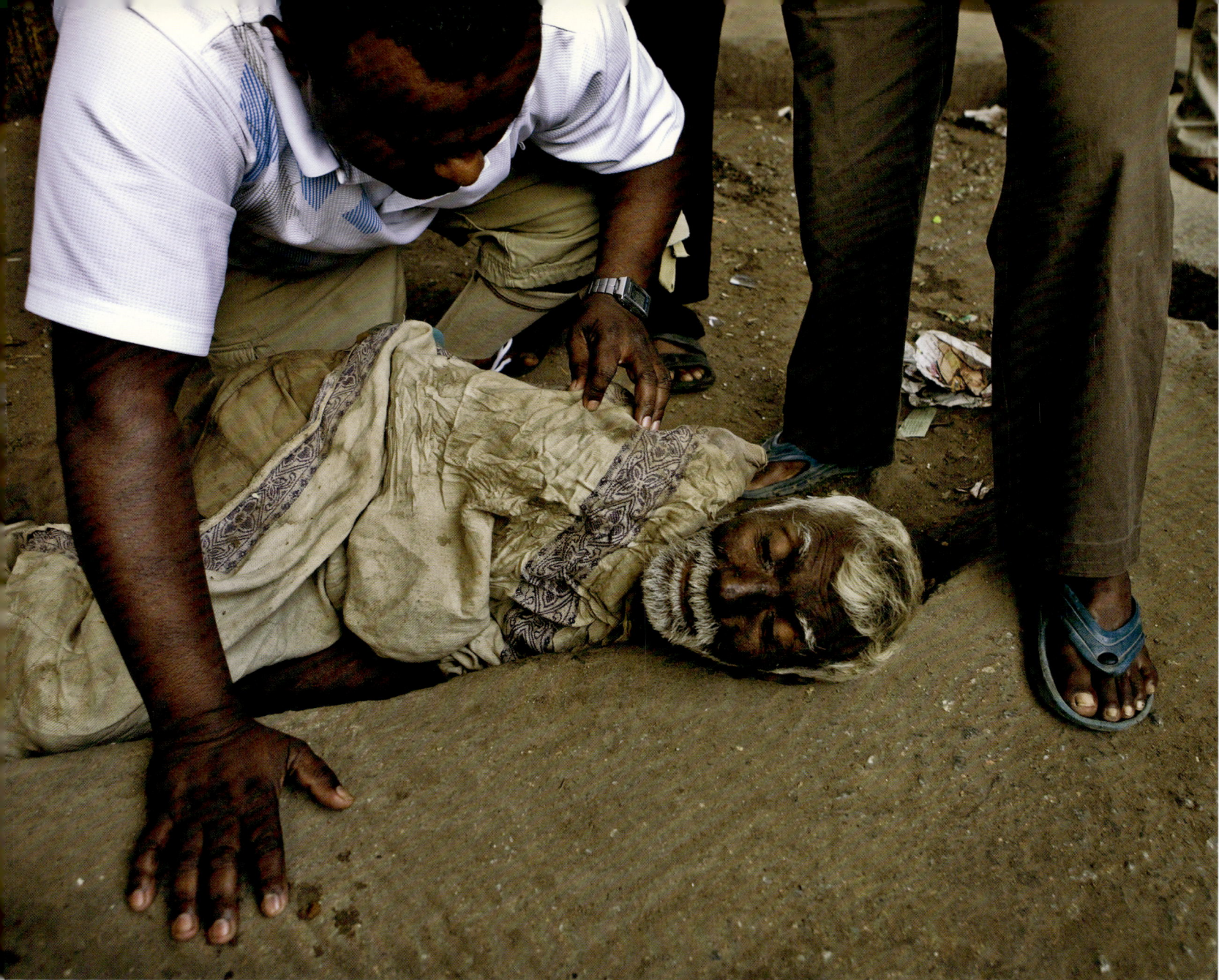

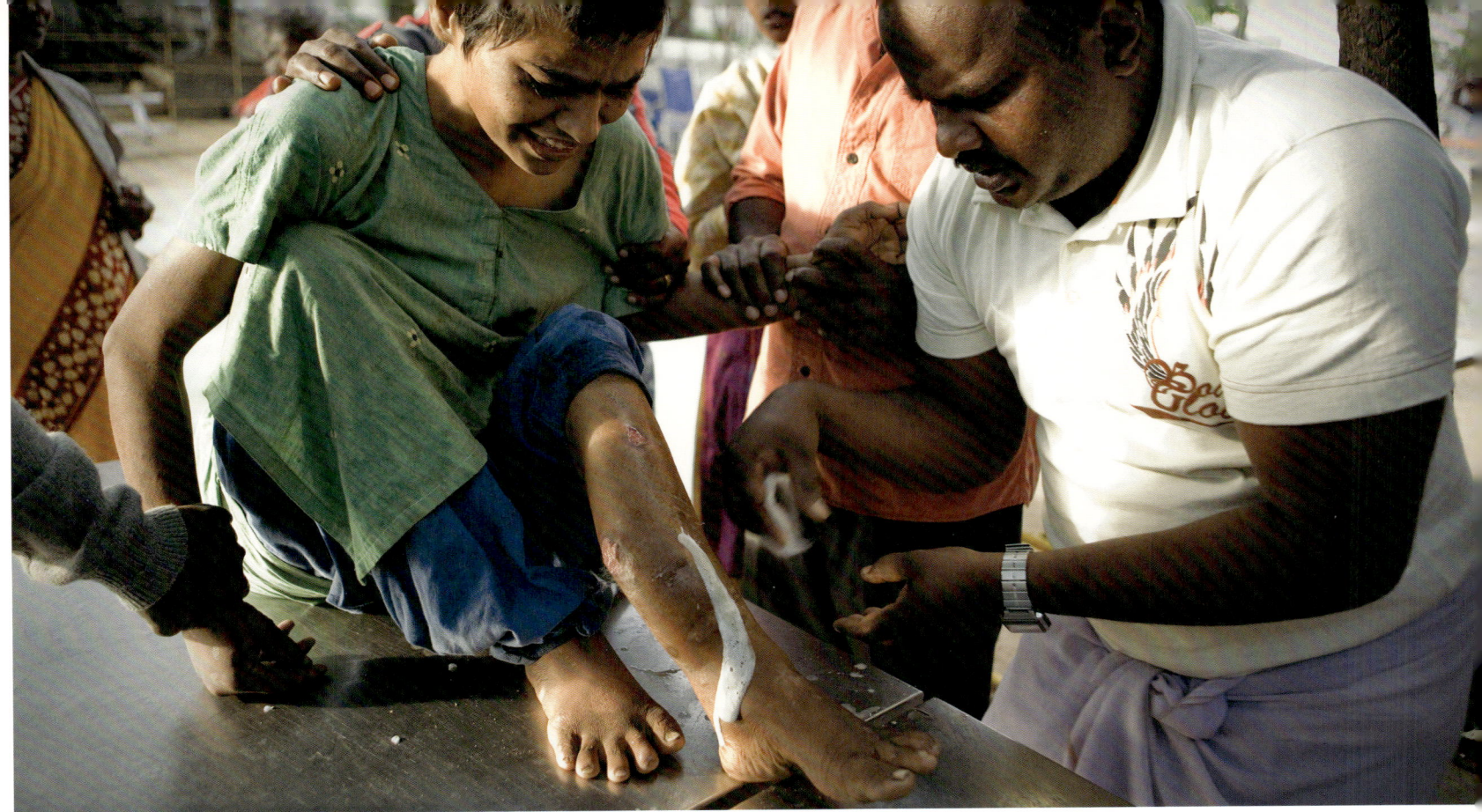

COMMUNITY
By Beatriz Barragan Horn

Space is a precious commodity throughout India. Due to the ever-expanding population and over-crowded urban centers, many citizens have begun to move out of the city to more rural areas.

LIGHT & LIFE ACADEMY
By Amanda Reyes

Iqbal K. Mohamed returned to India after graduating from Brooks Institute of Photography in the United States, and became one of India's leading advertising photographers. During the peak years of his career, Iqbal and his wife, Anuradha, decided to start the first professional photography institution in India: Light & Life Academy.

Light & Life Academy sits on a mountaintop in the Nilgiris Mountain Range in Tamil Nadu, India. Iqbal structured the curriculum around what he had learned at Brooks - improvising with the limited resources the school and India has to offer. Since India has so few photography stores that have the professional equipment needed, the students improvise, using construction paper and mirrors instead of expensive lights and other equipment. With these techniques, the students have learned to shoot an image under any circumstance.

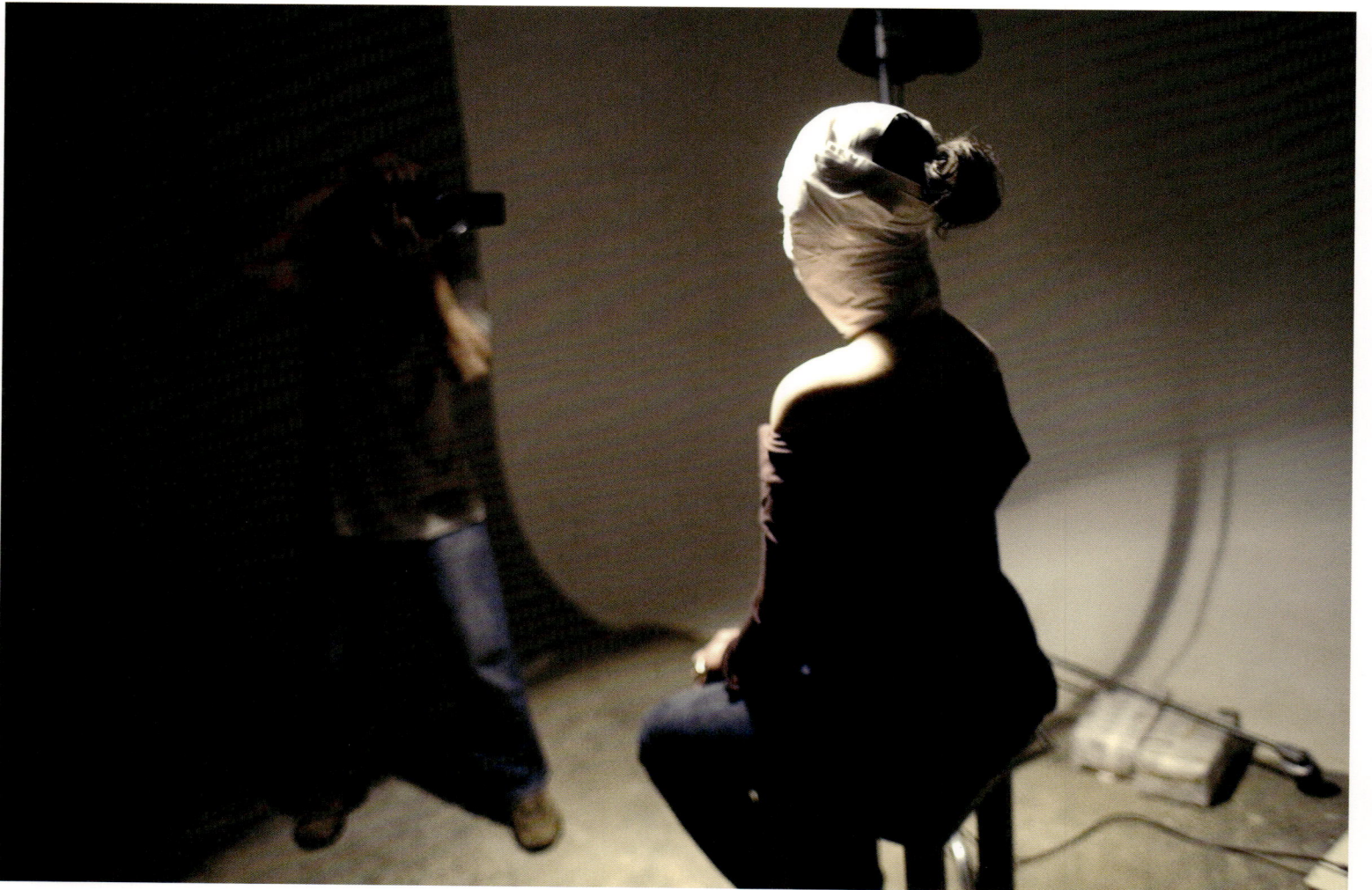

LAUGHTER

By Connie Myers

Children enjoy life's simple pleasures on the streets
of Bangalore, Karnataka.

RETURN OF THE TIGER

By Connie Myers

On December 3, 2008, after two attempts on his life, former Congress legislator, C.K. Jayachandra Reddy, who also goes by the name C.K. Babu, came out of his self-imposed, two-year exile.

It is rumored that Babu has been involved with numerous homicides and was even arrested under suspicion of murder in 2003, but later acquitted. Babu is now considered by many to be a champion of the people.

With impending elections, he led a rally from Chittoor to Gudipala to open the party office. Motorcycles and other vehicles, as well as hundreds on foot streamed in from neighboring villages. Supporters prepared a visual array of banners, posters, flags, firecrackers, and live bands to welcome Babu and show their allegiance to the political figure. During the procession, Babu, with his bodyguard's careful attention, accepted garlands from the heads of each village. The march continued on and ended at Gudipala, where Babu addressed the crowd. Speaking very frankly and holding true to his nickname, "The Chittoor Tiger," Babu declared his candidacy for the Chittoor assembly seat in the coming election.

ENDURANCE

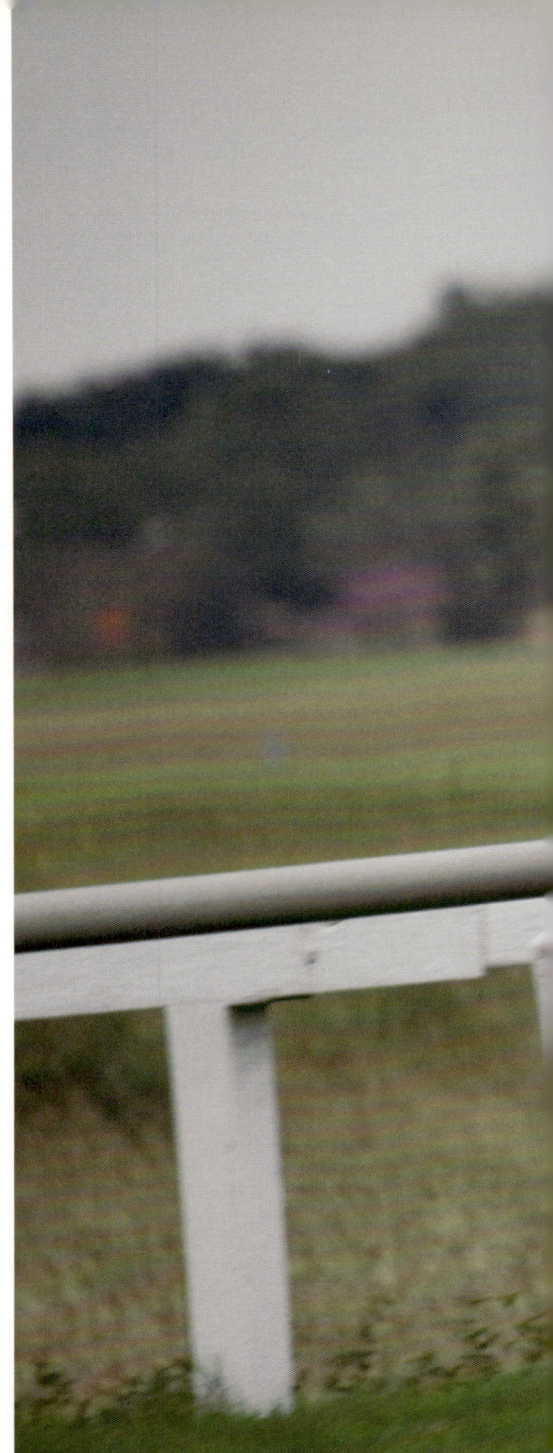

SPORT OF KINGS

By Joshua J. Anahonak, Rebecca Dornewass, Samantha Murphy & Madelynne Nehl

Crowds gather early at the local racetracks to judge a horse's form as it warms up before the race. Densely populated ticket windows bustle in the moments before the trumpet sounds. With the last bets made, adrenaline runs high as the crowd anxiously awaits the outcome. The crowd's roar echoes the thundering horses' hooves. At last, the race is over. The white cone is hoisted and the winner is made official. The victorious collect their winnings and the cycle begins again.

Horse racing in India has evolved from a recreational sport into an official business that draws in huge amounts of revenue. Commonly referred to as the "Sport of Kings," the majority of the profit comes from the gambling of the lower classes.

The sport can be extremely hard on the horses. Many of the races in India do not have age limits for the animals and it is common to run horses until the end of their life, usually between ten and 20 years old.

HOME OF LOVE

By Mia Shimabuku

"I think my father forgets me," says Vinitha Parthasarathy, reading a letter her father wrote from prison to her family at Home of Love in Chennai. "He'll write letters, but he will not ask about me. He only asks for my brother. He will not put my name on the letters, so I just cry. Sometimes I think I must hate my father."

On the outskirts of Chennai, in the village of Alamadhi, lives a 13-year-old named Vinitha Parthasarathy. Vinitha is a student and resident of Providence Residential Academy at Home of Love, an outreach program for young orphaned females.

At the age of ten, Vinitha was brought to Home of Love by her grandmother after she witnessed her father brutally murder her mother. During the three years she has spent at Home of Love, Vinitha has emerged as a student leader and is at the top of her class with a promising future ahead.

"All of the other children also hunger for that mother's love, so that's why I must love these children," Vinitha says.

Surrounded by the peace and love of her new home, Vinitha struggles to forget the scene of that fateful day and searches for forgiveness for her father.

PRESERVING THE PAST

By Adam Herrera

In a small four-room studio below street level in Chennai, a man works day and night to save India's past. Karthik V. is a commercial photographer by trade who also specializes in the restoration and archiving of historical photographs. About five years ago, Karthik opened Fine Grain Photography and Conservation, a photographic restoration company, to save some of India's most significant historical photographs before deterioration claimed them forever. His job is not an easy one, nor is it profitable, but if you ask Karthik why he insists on doing the work he simply replies, "because it needs to be done."

At this time, photographic conservation is virtually unheard of in India. "On a national level, no one knows that something can be done. No one knows that photographic safe-ty is possible. No one knows that these images can be protected," says Karthik.

Karthik and his staff work out of a small, 400 square-foot office that consists of a desk and chairs, a printing room, a developing room, and a drying room. The pipes are rusty, the faucet drips, and water damage blankets everything less than a foot off the ground. Because

of the temperate climate, much of the year the office and photographs are under threat from heat, humidity, and flood. "Last month we were hit with such force that the water table crept up and water was coming up through the floor, there was rain water coming in under the door, and we had water coming through the roof so we were forced to stop operations immediately," Karthik says.

However, the weather is not the only problem Karthik and his crew face while trying to preserve the images. Nearly all of the leading suppliers for traditional photography have pulled out of India, so

Karthik and his staff are forced to buy almost all of their photographic supplies from the US, UK, and Germany. Since they import their supplies, they must also pay the importation fees for each product, often costing them more than 100% of the actual retail price. In short, they pay double for everything.

Still, through all of the hardships Karthik and his staff have endured, they still manage to save thousands of historical images each year and produce some of the finest silver prints in the world. Currently, Fine Grain has shows traveling in galleries throughout Europe.

To date, Karthik has sunk to more than two million rupees (approx. $40,000) in debt trying to save India's photographic history. He now lives in a small three-bedroom home with his wife and two sons. With creditors knocking at his door, too few customers to pay the bills, and rising housing costs, Karthik fears he will soon have to move to a smaller, more affordable home.

A COCONUT LIFE

By Sybill Jecker

In the small village of Pathiyankara, near Kayamkulam Lake in the backwaters of Kerala, one family carries on a long tradition of harmony between the people and nature. There are many thriving industries unique to the backwaters environment, and among them is the harvesting of coconut palm trees. These trees are

an example of a 100% resource, meaning every component of the tree can be made into a useable product such as food, shelter, fuel and household items. Many families in this village thrive on the production of coir, a sturdy, water-resistant rope woven from the fibers of a coconut husk.

Ashish Lal, 12, lives with his mother, Kanchana, and his grandmother, Kaliyamma, in a house made of brick and woven coconut palm leaves. Various family members, including aunts, uncles and cousins, stroll in and out of the home daily, and contribute to meals and household chores. Kanchana and

Kaliyamma weave the coir that supports this family right in their front yard. For every 300 coir ropes produced (which takes about 8 hours working together), the women earn Rs 170 (less than $4) from a local cooperative society that then distributes the product throughout Kerala and other Indian states.

The family's special relationship with the local wildlife is a testament to the harmony that exists between man and nature, as a wild eagle often stops by to eat leftovers out of the hands of Ashish or Kanchana, and then hangs around to play with a ball that Ashish has thrown. The family pets also include a goat, a dog, and five ducks that are walked to a nearby pond in the morning and then gathered into a small pen near the home at night.

The simplicity of life in the backwaters is reflected in the laughter and peace that exists within the small communities of families and friends throughout the villages in this region. Living off the land that they share creates a bond that ties them all together.

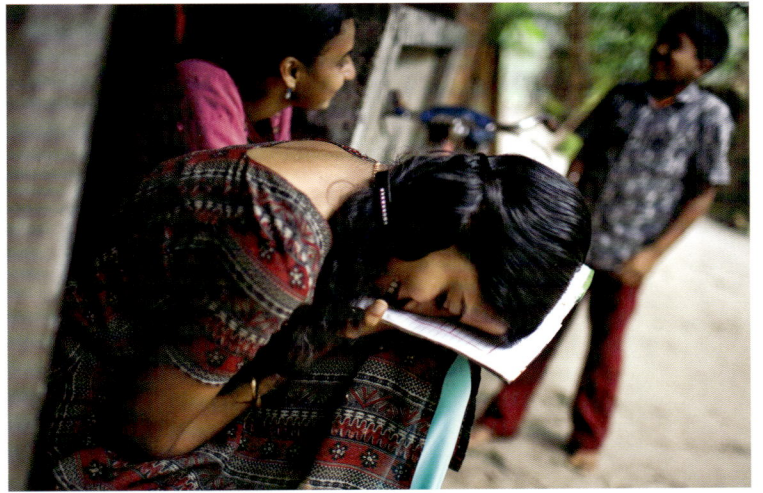

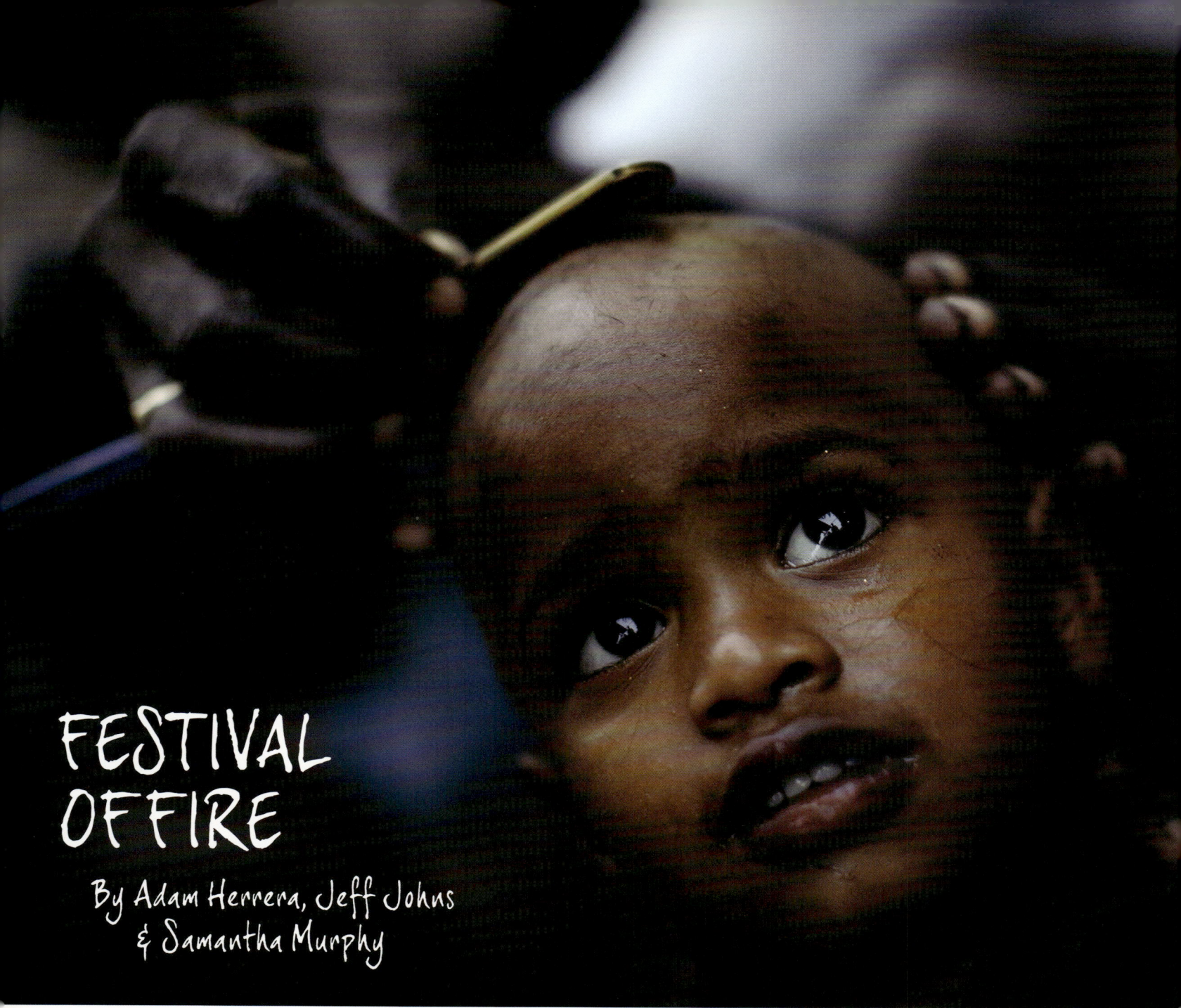

FESTIVAL OF FIRE

By Adam Herrera, Jeff Johns
& Samantha Murphy

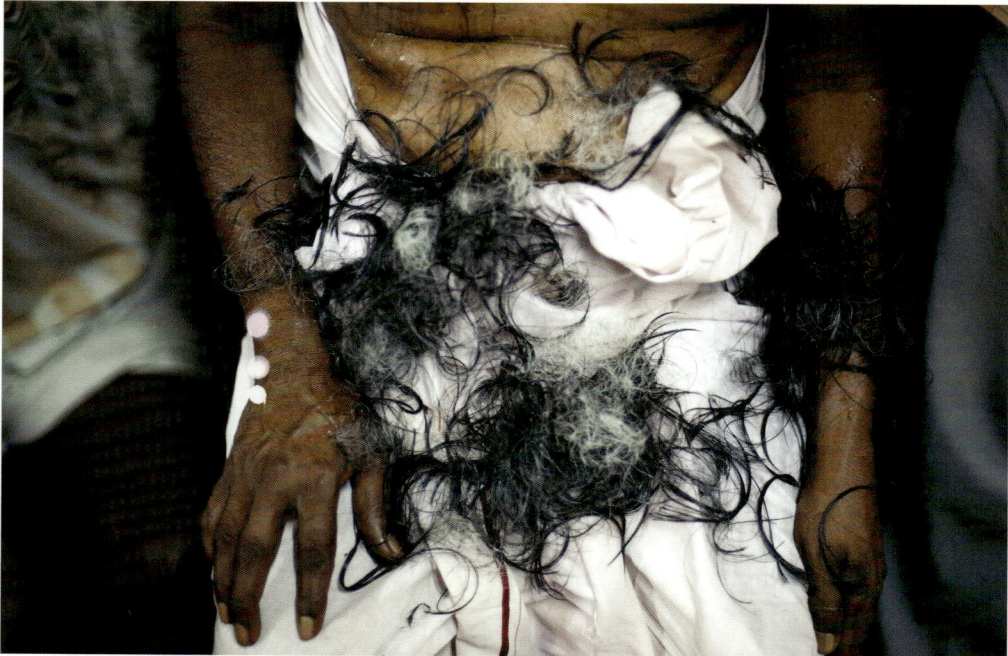

During the months of November and December, the small southern Indian town of Tiruvannamalai (Pop. 130,000), Tamil Nadu, draws nearly two million Hindu pilgrims from all over the world for the annual Karthikai Deepam festival.

The festival revolves around the belief that Shiva, the Hindu God of creation and destruction, appeared as an endless column of light to settle a dispute between Brahma and Krishna, the two other Gods in the Hindu Holy Trinity. At the request of his followers, Shiva, being too brilliant as a column of light, transformed himself into the mountain Arunachala.

Modern day Hindus who come to Tiruvannamalai for pilgrimage circle the mountain's 14 km base clockwise on foot. Many pilgrims also climb the summit where they worship Shiva at a large cauldron filled with 3,000 liters of ghee (clarified butter) that will burn for ten days with a wick of cotton cloths. This part of the journey is done barefoot to honor the holy spirit of the mountain.

The Hindu month of Karthik (around November and December) is observed by many Hindus by placing a small candle or lamp outside their front doors as a symbol of the flame on mount Arunachala.

The festival coincides with the full moon every year because the lunar cycle plays an important role in Hinduism. At 6:00 p.m. on the night of the full moon, all worshippers stop what they are doing and look to Arunachala in prayer as the cauldron is lit. The flame can be seen for up to ten miles away and the Arunachala temple complex, along with other Hindu temples in Tamil Nadu, line the night sky with flames in praise of Shiva, warding off evil forces and ushering in another year of prosperity.

HARMONY

By Cesare Naldi

In India, animals are revered as sacred beings and respected for their labor, throughout cities and the countryside. Entire lives are dedicated to these relationships and the serenity and love that is created can be seen in unexpected places.

THANK YOU

BROOKS INSTITUTE:
Roger Andersen (President) • Dale Angell (Faculty) • Glynn Beard (Film Program Director) • Susan Bloom (VJ Program Director) • Chris Buckpitt (Facility Manager Cota Street Campus) • Bruce Burkhardt (Faculty) • Donna Burr (Librarian) • Yvonne Check (Financial Aid) • John Christophers (Digital Lab Manager) • Greg Cooper (VJ Faculty) • Dan Emirzian (Faculty) • Barry Fagin (Ventura Checkout) • Adam Gerlach (Staff) • Nina Gomez (Marketing & Event Coordiator) • Ernie Greenwald (Groundskeeper) • Jesse Groves (Gallery Curator) • Joe Gosen (VJ Faculty) • Tim Halsey (Chief Financial Officer) • Steve Hamaker (Accounting) • Kari Ibarra (HR) • Bethany Innocenti (Manager of Alumni Relations, Art & Design) • Traci Jaslove (Mason St. Studio Manager) • Greg Lawler (Director, I.T.) • Paul Liebhardt (Faculty) • David Litschel (Provost) • David Lundgren (I.T.) • Russ McConnell (Faculty) • Barbara Obermeier (Faculty) • Chris Orwig (Faculty) • Brent Siebenaler (Staff) • Karin Stellwagen (Faculty) • Ban Yaw (I.T.) • Randal Zell (Accounting)

IN COUNTRY CONTACTS:
Sabita Currimbhoy • Shivani Dass • Ankit Goyal • Charan Hegde • Anuradha Iqbal • Rahul Jain • Garima Jain • Light & Life Academy • Lisu • Iqbal Mohamed • Mysore Race Club • Devaraja Market • Tusker Trail • IRS Agarbathi • Saif Ahmed & girlfriend Joyce • Babu • Kanan • Kumaran • Mohan & Everybody at Greenix • Raju • Sreeraj Pai • Sri Ramana Maharshi: John Maynard • Suresh • Rising Star Outreach • Becky Douglas • Vicki & Gordan Gibbs • Ron & Joyce Hanson • Dr. Karl & Amy Kirby • Dr. Senthil Kumar • Acha Kamath • Bangalore Turf Club • Bopy's Hotel • Chamraj Estate • Asha • Disha Barve • Ranjan Chacko • Crane Software Industries Corporation • John • Justin & Priya • The Karunya Community Development Ministries & Trust • Prem Khoshy • Kumar • Vivek Mathew • PFA- The People for Animals, Bangalore • Sam Pillai • Pradeep, VP • Rajan • Satish • Latha & Suresh Sigamani • Sunny & Shaun • Chandra Shekar • Sweety & Prince • The Art Village • Brinda • Satish Chakravarty • S. Das • Veena D'souza • N. Kathirvel • K . Kumar • Andrew Vasanth-Louis • S. Malathy • S. Maneshwar • Nadasan • Manasi Parekh • G. Rangaraj • Satymoorty • N. Sivakumar • S. Suresh • Jebastian Raj • Liza Behrendt, Beauty of Water • Md Faiz, Cogent • Rajeev Gopal, Ghandi Study Circle • Dr. Rani Kamalan • Muthu Kumaran • Dr. Rajkumar Reghunathan & Susan Flint-Rajkumar • Rajeev Jose • Casabianca • Kanchana & Kaliyamma • Schrya Surendran, Sivananda Yoga Vedanta Centre • Babu Varghese, Tourindia • Min Ameen • Chali Grinnell • Vinodhini Joshi • Noel Parent • Mauna van der Vlugh • Kabali • Balan • Courtyard by Marriott, Chennai • Pastor Solomon & Clara Prabhakaran • Gospel Lighthouse Church • M.P.A Church • Pastor Devasitham, Suguna • Raga at Hotel Kakshimi • The Coffee Inn • Philipkutty's Farm: Anu Mathew • Mr. Steven: Little Angels Children's House • Dhilip: Stone Gallery • D. Baba Nowaraj: Tea Plantation Factory Manager • Connemara Tea Plantation • Ashok Kumar K. • Selvam P. • Noah • All India Christian Council • Mr. and Mrs. Dhanapal Moses • Sam Joseph • Home of Love • New Ark Mission of India • Vinitha Parasarathy • Sam Paul • T. Raja (Thomas) • Mithra Satuluri • Kumar Swamy • Paul Vedamuthu • Wilma Rodriguez • Saahas (Waste Management NGO in Bangalore) • Vijaya Shenoy • Ravi Agarwal (Photographer Contact For Saahas) • E-WaRDD • Electronic and Electrical Waste Recycling Dismantling and Disposal • Asif Pasha • EMPA • Materials Science and Technology • Luc Brondel (M. Sc. Environmental Engineer EPFL) • Swiss Indian E-waste Project • Sree Lakshmi Enterprises • Waste Paper & Raw Material Suppliers • G. Ravi Kumar (Manager & Owner) • B.K. Venkatesh Raju (Manager and Owner) • Mythri Sarva Seva Samithi (Non-Profit Society working with slums in Bangalore) • Pramila (Field Worker) • Saraswathi (Ragpicker from the Cement Colony) • South Indian Railways • Indian Railways Fan Club Association • S. Venkataraaman • Velmurugan • K. Shankar, Manjula, Gokul, Vasanth • Vishkanta • Mapunity • Ashwin Mahesh (Professor at Institute of Management & Traffic Analyst for Mapunity.com) • Allergy Asthma ENT Clinic • Dr. Pendakur Anand • Rahul Brown (Contact for Sean Blagsvedt) • Babajob.com (Social Networking Website for Employment) • Sean Olin Blagsvedt (Co-Founder) • Shrutti Salghur(Human Resources Manager), Janardhan Salghur, Shailaja Salghur, Krutika "Amu" Salghur, Nikhil "Niki" Salghur • Deepa B • Gracy Mary P. • Asha • Mrs. Jeena Prakash • Deepak Gulati • S. Vinod • Shyla Cariappa • Manjula • Electronic City • Aman Tyagi • Amandeep Singh • Ismali Mohammed • Nesamalar Blind Orchestra Troop • Blind & Handicapped Service Center • Saminathan (Treasurer) • Dr. Mahendra Shrestha (Program Director, International Tiger Coalition) • Dr. Ajith Kumar (Center for Wildlife Studies & National Center for Biological Studies) • Sanjay Gubbi (Assistant Director, Wildlife Conservation Society of India) • Dr. Ravi Chellam (Country Director, Wildlife Conservation Society of India) • Karthik V. (Fine Grain Photography & Conservation) • P.M. Muthanna (Conservation Fellow, Wildlife Conservation Society of India) • Pandurangaswamy T. (LIFT Project) • Minal • Sparsa Hotel manager, S. Laxminarayan • Sreeraj Vai • Mr. Vinkatesan

ADDITIONAL THANKS:
Martin Alphonse • Karin Horn de Barragan • Courtney Beckett • Victoria Black • Brian Brantley • Olga Martin del Campo • Gauri Chopra • Ashley Conde • Door of Faith • Kelly Dusenbury • Tania Guzman • Haggai Institute • Barbara Holman • Robert & Judy Homsher • Rafael Barragan Horn • Sus & Karen Imoto • Ireland Group • Julia Johns • Todd & Sheila Johns • Krishna • Brandy Laidler • Michael Lewis • Diane Lundgren • Rafael Barragan Maldonado • Bob & Peggy Martinez • Matt McLoone • Liesl Messerlie • Russ Morrissey • Chase Murphy • Daniel Murphy • Karen Myers • Steven Myers • Dawn Neal • Frank & Margie Newell • Michelle Newell • Alison Ogunseitan • Port Graham Village • Sierra Prescott • Ronin & Rimmi • Bill & Patricia Steinmetz • Venita De Souza • Norma & Claus Stengel • Dr. Angela Sutter • Jacqueline Utterback • Beatriz Batiz Vidrio • Ke Aha Vineyard • John Waskey • Zachary Reed Watkins • Alexandra Webber • Bill & Stella Webber • Christian Weissert • Lilianne Wenger • Rob Winner

ADDITIONAL SUPPORT:

Ray Acevedo (Olympus) • Jen Colucci (Senior Public Relations Coordinator, Olympus) • Lucas Deming • Dr. Mary Dial • Gail Duncan (Kodak) • Christian Erhardt (Director of Marketing, Photographic Division, Leica Cameras Inc.) • Brian Erwin (Think Tank Photo) • Dr. Linda Fickes • Lesley Foster • John Huber • Ebi & Mary Jo Kuehne (Leica Cameras Inc, Southern California District) • Tali Miller • Jon Moeller (Digital Fusion) • Doug Murdoch (Product Designer/President, ThinkTankPhoto.com) • Jaideep Oberoi • Brock Potter • Tony Stanfield • Jenning Steger (Photo Editor, Patagonia) • Aaron Vogel • Jason Young (Absolute Rentals)

PRESALE SUPPORT:

Laura Adam • George Ameel • Darlene Anahonak • Roger Andersen • Darla Anderson • Virginia Anderson • Teri Andrs • Diane Amott • LeBurta Atherton • Jeff Baker • Jake Barker • William Bartholomay • Virginia Bartholomay • Kathy Beam • Gene A. Beery • Betsy Benoit • James Benoit • Martin Bick • Larry Bishop • Bud Black • Stephen & Delores Black • Susan Bloom • Stephanie Bollaert • Julie Boruta • Andrei Boudreau • Mary Bozeman • Robert Bradshaw • Isolde Braun • Balbi Brooks • Kim Brower • Evelyn Tachau-Brown • Petra Bruning • Sara Burbidge • Bruce Burkhardt • Cheryl Burger • Roger Burghdoff • Dana Burghdoff • Keegan Burris • Rick & Karen Burton • Brown Cannon • Felica Caplan • Iris Kimura Carpio • Richard & Karen Cavender • Alexandria Cesena • Balam Chavez • Cate Chavez • Isabel Chavez • Daniel Smith/Yvonne Check • Brian Cheyne • Star Chow • Ralph Clevenger • Geoffery Close • Greg Cooper • Laura Costa • David Cross • Sandy Davidson • Nick Dekker • Dean DePhillipo • John Dolan • Robin Dornewass • Stephen Dornewass • Sally Downey • Eric Dowry • Jeff Dunn • Charlene Ebright • Mike Eckelkamp • Bradley Edward • Rhonda Ferguson • Mitchell Fedewa • Alicia Fenning • Kathleen Fenning • Nancy Fenning • Linda Fickes • Stephen Fish • Shayna Fitzgerald • Kirby Fong • Heather Fortinberry • Christine Funk • Joe Gantz • Dan Gardner • John Gates • Valerie Gates • Miki Gavin • Ron Gima • Reba Gonzales • Augustin Gonzalez • Jack Gosen • Donna Granata • Dave Grant • Sierra Green • Duffy Griffin • Richard Gunner • Barbara Hahon • Christine Hahn • Lewis Haidt • Judy Haller • Deborah Hargus • Brian Harper • Jeff & Rita Harrigan • Chris & Vivian Hartenau • Penny Harvey • Curtis Lee Hebert • John Hendrick • Kieran Henthorn • Irene & Paul Herrera • Lindsay Herrera • Robert Herrera • Solomon Hill • Dave & Barbara Holman • E. Alison Holman • Hal & Diana Holman • Mike Holman • Donna Homsher • Jack Hooven • Jean Horton • Marguerite Howe • Marti Howe • Tri Huynh • Kari Ibarra • Jenny Inge • Sue Jahnke • Daniel Jauregui • Travis Jecker • M. Craig Johns • Todd Johns • Elise & Ryan Johnson • Shelley Johnson • Larry Kairaiuak • David Kinnaman • Diane Kordich • Erinn Kredba • WM Kuhlke • Tracy Lamee • Brandy Laidler • Greg Lawler • Tamara Lar • Margaret Lee • Blake Lewis • Kenneth Lewis • Shaana Lichty • Stephanie Lindloff • David Litschel • Michael Logan • Tom Loge • Corky Lorcorran • Ryan Loughridge • Diane Lundgren • Kelly Maddalena • John Mahoney • Mary Malchoff • David Malchoff • Donna Malchoff • Vivian Malchoff • Alexander Manning • Kathy Manning • Samantha Marinaro • Lissa Matsumoto • Deb Mattley • Tui McCarthy • Brandon McCarty • Amanda McCarver • Kathy McKulin • Matt McLoone • Jim McNay • Deborah McNeil-Amorteguy • Sheena McOuat • Nate Medina • Ismael Medrano • Suzie Mein • Peggy Miklebach • Scott Miles • Justin Miller • Joyce Millstead • Keith Moffatt • Beth & Rob Molzahn • Jenna Moran • Russ Morrissey • Lara Mueting • Emma Murphy • Albert Myers • David Myers • Thomas and Kathy Myers • Michelle Myers • Valerie Myers • Jane Nakatani • Kailash Narayan • Dana Nearburg • Annemarie Nehl • Cecillia Nehl • Thomas Nehl • Jennifer Nelson • Aimee Newell • Margie Newell • Michelle Newell • Ted Nieters • Paul & Luanne Oleas • Barbara Olson • Brian C. Olson • Ann Ono • Gail Osherenko • Jeremy Ota • Kevin Ott • Brianna Owens • Lisa Pack • Irma Reyes Panduro • Kathy Papazian • Chloe Pastori • Mike Petersen • Denese Phillips • Bonnie Pierce • Season Pineda • Chuck Place • Nancy Pulliam • Marilyn Purdy • Reginald Ramirez • Anacleto & Terrie Rapping • Carolyn Terry • Emily Ray • Cindy Reed • Shelia Reed • Elaine Reese • Sue Reese • Kevin Reese • Alicia Reiner • Andrea Reyes • Carlos & Erika Reyes • Hector Reyes • Damian Richardson • Linda Rodesky • Fred Rudd • Mike Ruocco • Gloria Sato • Anne Salomon • Carol Schiro • Nini Seaman • Kim Seefeld • Christine Seville • Jerlyn Ray Shelley • Lisa Shimabuku • Susan Shiras • David Shirk & Alexandra Webber • Kirsten Silva • Sireenah Siman • Betty & Mike Simpson • Paul & Jan Sirkin • Noah Smukler • Curtis Solberg • Juliet Sponsel • Fay Stafford • Kimberlee Staking • Claus Stengel • Peter Storm • Joanne Struebing • Renee Stynchula • Kimberly A. Sullivan • Michele & Chuck Susie • Angela E. Sutter • Robert Swanland • Raymond Swanland • Shelley Swanland • Ken Swantz • Mrs. Phelps H. Swift • Denis Theroux • John & Anzie Thomas • Erin Tice • Johanna Torkelson • Jenna Tower • Pam Treadwell • Tracy Trotter • Chandra Uber • Vincent Van Gogh • Roberta Villavecchia • Bryant Vinisky • Rob Vinisky • Steve Vinisky • Kelley Virkicheuh • Greg Voight • Bern Wagner • Margaret Wagner • Diane Wallach • Scott Watts • Stella Webber • Hugh & Janet Weber • Eric Wells • Alex Wells • Fran & Tony West • Noel West • Bethine Whitney • Alec Wikczynski • Gail Williams • Tim Williams • Karina Wise • Jimmy Wilson • Jennifer Wilson • Scott Woodruff • Harry Yakabe • Charles Yakabe • Annette Yamada • Naomi Yamashiro • Lorie Yanuaria

THE PHOTOGRAPHERS

Josh Anahonak, 20
Port Graham, Alaska
Visual Journalism

"My family and other people I know is what inspires me. When I am out in the field I start looking for what they would like to see and that changes my perspective in the current environment."

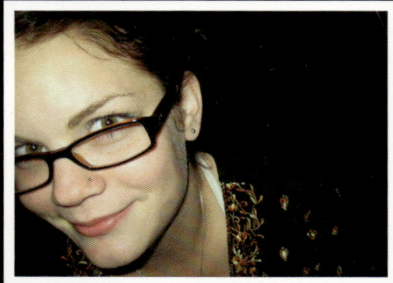

Courtney Black, 20
Haifa, Israel
Professional Photography

"Daily events and occurrences are my inspiration. Whether it's seeing new places or capturing the union of marriage, it's the adventures in life that make it worthwhile."

Rebecca Dornewass, 22
Williamstown, New Jersey
Professional Photography

"Life inspires me."

Alana Fickes, 20
Honolulu, Hawaii
Film & Video Production

"People inspire me. I love seeing a person really being creative and coming to life. It motivates me to share their passion with others."

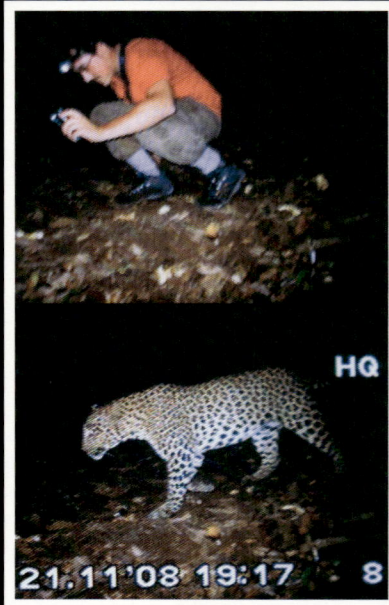

Adam Herrera, 17
Grand Ledge, Michigan
Professional Photography

"Discovery inspires. I both love and hate the fact that there are countless things to discover in this world. I love the idea that there are forgotten, or lost places waiting to be rediscovered in nearly every corner of the globe, but I hate the fact that no matter how hard I try, I will never be able to see them all before I die. I try to use my photography to both remind people of the amazing places that surround them, and to inspire them to venture out and discover these places for themselves."

Jennifer Homsher, 37
Creede, Colorado
Professional Photography

"Capturing the beauty in every moment is what inspires me; challenges me."

Beatriz Barragan Horn, 23
Guadalajara, Mexico
Film & Video Production

"The one thing that inspires me the most as a documentarian is: Global Warming. Making people aware that each action counts towards sustainable living."

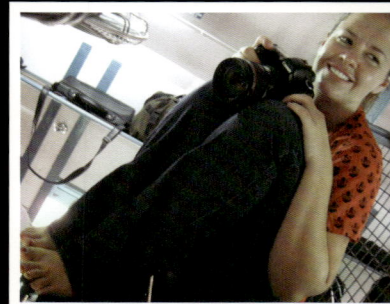

Sybill Jecker, 32
San Luis Obispo, California
Visual Journalism

"My sons, Kelby and Kyler, inspire me to be a better person every day and chase my dreams so that I can teach them to do the same."

Jeff Johns, 24
Washington, D.C.
Visual Journalism

"The idea that I can capture an image that no one will ever be able to capture again. That's exciting!"

Samantha Murphy, 21
Lake Bluff, Illinois
Professional Photography

"The opportunity to create something unique, something that has depth and conveys emotion, is what really inspires me."

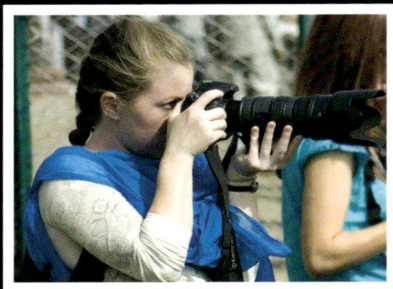

Connie Myers, 17
San Diego, California
Professional Photography

"One thing that inspires me with photography is the ability to make time stand still."

Cesare Naldi, 31
Napoli, Italy
Professional Photography

"The thing that inspires me most is the ability of killing time, or in other words the ability of making an instant eternal."

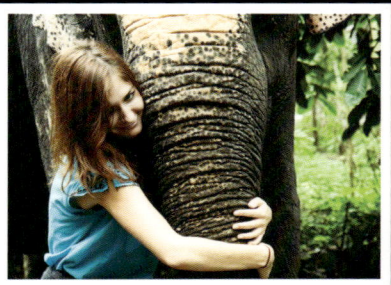

Madelynne Nehl, 20
Shelby Township, Michigan
Professional Photography

"I find inspiration in everything. Everyday experiences are my creative fuel."

Stephanie Newell, 28
Long Beach, California
Visual Journalism

"I am inspired by the unfamiliar. I am inspired by different traditions, cultures, religions, and conflicts. I am inspired by the immense diversity of the human condition."

Amanda Reyes, 21
Monrovia, California
Professional Photography

"My inspiration comes from my passion to see and experience new things. This journey through India has given my photography the direction I have been searching for."

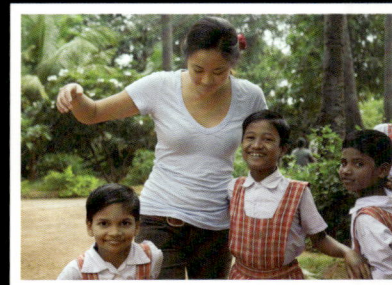

Mia Shimabuku, 20
Kahului, Hawaii
Visual Journalism

"Photography sparks my questions and makes me look for the answers. The challenge to see and feel at the same time, while living someone else's life for a fraction of a second, is all I know about it...so far..."

Janine Stengel, 22
Munich, Germany
Visual Journalism

"Every moment breathes gestures and circumstances for hungry eyes to be explored. A second look helps you educate."

Nicole Vinisky, 21
Sherwood, Oregon
Professional Photography

"As a photographer I am inspired by my family. They have been my struggle, comfort, and push through my work."

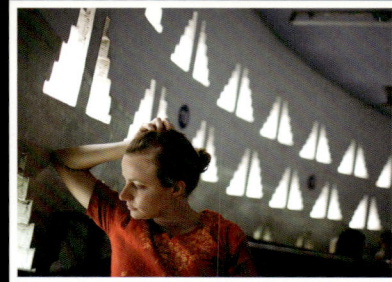

Ellen Webber, 31
Los Angeles, California
Visual Journalism

"People inspire me: creating narratives, capturing moments, interpreting moods, exploring thoughts, wandering the earth and seeing life through my veil and others."

Serena Wells, 34
Garberville, California
Visual Journalism

"What inspires me as a photographer...beautiful things, old architecture, a person's smile, the changing colors of the leaves, the way a person moves or looks at that moment, a color, a mood...it changes all the time."

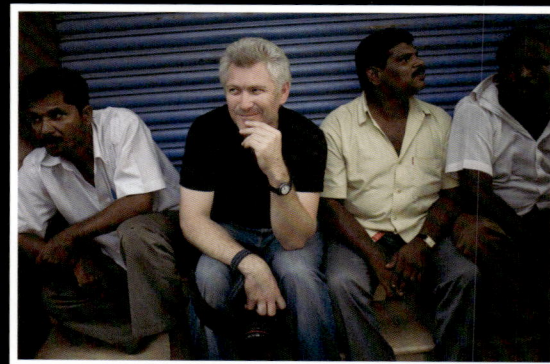

Paul Myers, 35
San Jose, California
Faculty, Visual Journalism

"A bit of light, some laughter, the street... these are a few of the things that drive me to photograph."